# LANCASTER'S
# *Historic inns*

First published in 2009
by Palatine Books,
Carnegie House,
Chatsworth Road
Lancaster LA1 4SL
www.palatinebooks.com

British Library Cataloguing-in-Publication data
A catalogue record for this book is available from the British Library

ISBN: 978-1-874181-28-6

Designed and typeset by Carnegie Book Production
www.carnegiebookproduction.com
Printed and bound in the UK by Short Run Press, Exeter

# LANCASTER'S
# *Historic inns*

## ANDREW WHITE

# *Acknowledgements*

*T*HIS BOOK COULD NOT have been written without the active support of many. First of all, those predecessors on the same trail, especially the late Eija Kennerley and Keith Greenhalgh, who brought much-needed academic rigour to a field which is often based upon hearsay and half-truth. Ken Ineson has been very helpful, especially in allowing me to copy the list of inns used for election entertainment in 1772. My former colleagues at Lancaster City Museums, Susan Ashworth, Paul Thompson, Andy Hornby, Wendy Moore and Ivan Frontani, have all helped in innumerable ways, while a long sequence of volunteers have transcribed details from Trade Directories. Staff of the Lancashire Library Service in Lancaster Central Library Reference Department, such as Jenni Loveridge and Susan Wilson, have pulled out obscure handbills and scrapbooks for me, while at the Lancashire Record Office I owe a debt of gratitude to Andrew Thynne for giving me access to various wills and recognisances. I am grateful to other colleagues at the Cumbria Record Office at Barrow-in-Furness for permission to use the splendid Soulby Collection of handbills in their care. At Lancaster University I particularly single out Dr Michael Winstanley for help with the story of the exchange of licenses between old central pubs and new suburban ones in the late Victorian period. Julia Stables, MA student there in 1999, carried out useful work on the 1881 census and the role of women in public houses.

Finally, thank you to Alistair, Anna and Lucy at Carnegie Publishing for daring to publish this book, and for help at various stages.

# *Contents*

The *Sun Inn*, built on its present site in 1785, but successor to a much older inn of the same name on an adjacent site, demolished to create the Sun Street development.

# Introduction

Lthough I have known inns all my life and
sampled a great many, my introduction to Lancaster's inns came
in 1967 when as an 18 year-old undergraduate arriving in the city
I came to know their finer points as only a student can.

Our favoured drinking-place then was the *Shakespeare Hotel* in St
Leonardgate (sometimes spelt St Leonardsgate or St Leonard's Gate), a
short stagger from the University's base at St Leonard's House (Bailrigg
was still mostly a building site). Here the landlord had an amazing
knack after just one visit of remembering your name and favoured drink,
immensely flattering to those young and arrogant intellectuals, who felt
that their outstanding personalities were at last being recognised, and no
doubt quite financially advantageous to him as well. The *Shakespeare* was
not just a drinking-place but a base from which to consider where to go
next, to meet friends, or attend various clubs such as the Folk Club which
met in its upstairs room.

Of course it was not the only inn we favoured with our custom, and as
time went on the range widened. Morecambe was not forgotten, while the
*Golden Ball* at Snatchems or the *Royal* at Heysham were both popular.
For those with transport the rural delights of the *Bridge Inn* at Tatham
Bridge, famous for its lack of beer engines, enticed the visitor with the
novelty of having beer brought in a jug from the cellar. Even more fun
was the realisation that they used an approximately one-litre jug to bring
up beer, so that if you asked for two pints they had to make another
journey.

At that time many Lancaster pubs consisted of a multitude of small
rooms and alcoves, with fixed bench seating, upholstered in red leather,
and waiter service. But for those who bemoan the loss of such character this was only one layer in a complex history. And it was not just
the interiors which have changed over the centuries. The above is just
the perspective of some forty years. Many Lancaster inns have histories
going back at least two centuries. The uses have also changed and so has
the clientele. While there may be a few 'rough' pubs still remaining it is
doubtful whether we can produce today pubs of the established villainy of

Inn sign for the *Shakespeare*, now a hotel, but in the mid 1960s the favourite pub for students at the new Lancaster University.

those which once stood in China Lane and Bridge Lane, such as the *Hole in the Wall* or the *Volunteer*, where Victorian policemen called with great reluctance and in force when they needed to extract a particular villain. The licensing process, criticised as it is, has removed most of the worst offenders. Now much the same concerns are voiced about night clubs.

What is it about pubs that we continue to like? After deep reflection, lasting all of about thirty seconds, I think the enduring appeal is due to our ability to go into one, to eat or drink if we want, to talk if we want, or not to talk, to be on neutral territory where we can relax and stay if we want, or go if we want. And on the whole one can be quite an odd character before anyone takes any notice! There is always a particular pleasure in going into a pub as a group after some vigorous activity, and carrying out the usual post-mortem on what went wrong and who was responsible. One of my particular pleasures is that of trying to guess what a particular group of strangers has in common. There is a fascinating mix of anonymity and familiarity in such places.

Not everyone looks on pubs with pleasure. At their worst they can be sources of rowdiness and even violence, nor is there anything new in this. At various times there have been concerted efforts by certain groups to get rid of them entirely, or at least to diminish their influence. The Temperance movement was just the largest and most successful of these, but where is it now? We have seen the same approach to smoking and litter in our own time, although the smoking ban in public places seems to have been reasonably effective. It has been seen as a paternalistic move by the middle classes but not everyone involved was just out to restrict the working man's opportunities for getting drunk. There was a serious social issue when to be married to, or the child of, a boozer was to be in danger of want, starvation or even violent death. Magistrates, councillors and police made common cause over the worst offending pubs in the town centre and at least sought to have their licenses transferred to a new breed of 'respectable' hotels in the suburbs.

In these pages I look at various aspects of the public house and its culture in Lancaster. The buildings themselves, the landlords, the services they provided, and the resistance they provoked from time to time are all of interest to the social historian as well as the modern user. There is also a consideration of how we know what we know, what the sources of information are, and how we might reconstruct the inns of a former era. Many inns have a long history and those that don't, quickly invent one. History sells, in this business.

Fashions change very rapidly in this field, and the names of city-centre pubs, favourite drinks, type of clientele and many other facets of pub culture have moved on markedly even while I have been researching and writing this. Undoubtedly, some parts of it will already be out-of-date at the time of publication.

Finally, here are two quotations, illustrating the two extremes in outlook on the subject of inns. Both have the merit of still being true.

> The vile obscene talk, noise, nonsense and ribaldry discourses together with the fumes of tobacco, belchings and other foul breakings of wind, that are generally found in an ale-room … are enough to make any rational creature amongst them almost ashamed of his being. But all this the rude rabble esteem the highest degree of happiness and run themselves into the greatest straits imaginable to attain it.
>
> *A Dissertation upon Drunkenness*, 1727

> There is nothing which has yet been contrived by man, by which so much happiness is produced as by a good tavern or inn.
>
> Dr Johnson, 1776

STAIRCASE IN THE KING'S ARMS.

Interior of *King's Arms Hotel* from a mid-nineteenth-century woodcut.

CHAPTER ONE

# Inn Services

## Travellers

UNTIL THE LATE NINETEENTH CENTURY travellers had little alternative than to stay at an inn of some sort. There were many levels of accommodation available, ranging from the occupation of the whole inn by a particularly smart family and its entourage, down to occupation of the inn kitchen by the poorer travellers or servants accompanying their employers. In between these extremes the quality of room and service one received would be determined by how busy the inn was and one's apparent status. Pastor Moritz, a German clergyman who insisted on walking around England in 1782, was treated uniformly badly by innkeepers who could not conceive that a respectable man would choose to be a pedestrian. (C. P. Moritz, *Travels in England in 1782*, 1887) Whoever one might be; it was a bad idea to arrive on a fair or market day, or when the Assizes were on.

There are many descriptions of Lancaster by travellers, between the sixteenth and the twentieth centuries. Many of these also described their inn, usually in a summary fashion but occasionally in more detail.

### 1634 Capt. William Howard

... We entred into the famous County Palatine of Lancaster by a fayre, lofty, long Archt Bridge, over the river Lun, wee were for the *George* in Lancaster, and our Host was the better acquainted with the Affayres of the Shire, for that his Brother [Mr. Covile] was bothe a Justice of the Peace and a cheife Gaoler there ... and although our Host was a good Informer, yet he was a surley, and a touchy Lad, rotten he was I thinke, and so was our Hostesse, as by her behaviour at Table appear'd, witnesse my fellow Travellers ...

(L. G. Wickham Legg (ed.), *A Relation of a Short Survey of 26 Counties observed in a seven weeks Journey begun on August 11, 1634, by a Captain, a Lieutenant and an Ancient*, 1904, 43–4)

### 1705 Joseph Taylor

... about nine we arriv'd at Lancaster, and set up at the *Sun*, where we lay all night.

(W. Cowan (ed.), *A Journey to Edenborough in Scotland by Joseph Taylor, Late of the Inner Temple, Esq.* (1705), 1903, 161)

### 1745 Lady Oxford

June 1, Saturday ... from thence fourteen miles to Lancaster to the "*Sun*", a good Inn.

(*Historical Manuscripts Commission, Dukes of Portland*, VI, 1901, 190)

### 1759 John Crofts

... The *Sun* is a very decent inn ...

(B. G. Hutton, 'A Lakeland journey, 1759', *Cumberland & Westmorland Antiquarian & Archaeological Society*, 2nd ser., LXI, 1961, 290)

### 1769 Thomas Gray

Lancaster also appeared very conspicuous and fine; for its most distinguished features, the castle and church, mounted on a green eminence, were all that could be seen. Woe is me! when I got thither, it was the second day of their fair; the inn, in the principal street, was a great old gloomy house, full of people; but I found tolerable quarters, and even slept two nights in peace ...

(quoted in T. West, *Guide to the Lakes*, 1793, 217–19)

### 1795 Rev. William MacRitchie

... Put up at the *King's Arms* (Coulthwaite), and sup with a Mr. Lapworth from Coventry ... After supper, at the table of a kind, hospitable landlord return to the King's Arms, and enjoy four hours of slumber.

(Rev. W. MacRitchie, *Diary of a Tour through Great Britain*, 1897, 36)

### 1804 Millicent Bant

... Lancaster *Whitehart Inn* – very reasonable & Civil people – Gave us an excellent dinner & desert ...

(Essex Record Office, D/DFR F1)

## 1808 Richard Holden

... A bad Town, narrow streets, crowded, the Market day – a dirty Inn ...

(Rotherham Central Library 2/FI/1)

## 1816 William Monson

... The Inn at Lancaster is the *King's Arms*, very good & civil attendance; they have a curious custom in Lancashire beside the dinner ordered they load the table with all the productions of the house, cold meat, fowls, tarts &c &c without charge for it cheaper than one dish costs in town ...

(Lincolnshire Archives Office, Monson 15/B/2 ff12–14)

## 1818 Rev. Benjamin Newton

... We arrived at the *King's Arms*, the most magnificent inn in appearance of any we have entered since we left home ... Mrs. Pritt the landlady a very civil nice woman and the inn very comfortable but the charge for beds and breakfast higher than anywhere since we have been out ...

(C. P. Fendall and E. A. Crutchley, *The Diary of Benjamin Newton Rector of Wath 1816–1818*, 1933, 203–4)

## 1835 Sir George Head

In a humour, the first moment of landing, to be out of conceit with my present quarters – in due course, as I proceeded up the town, I found more reasonable grounds of dissatisfaction, and particularly when on requesting an apartment in the principal inn [the *King's Arms*], I was conducted to the garrets. The assizes were unluckily on that very day at their zenith: a festival, of which the signs and phenomena below stairs, and in the streets, were apparent; – bloated country coachmen, in their best liveries, stood lounging in the stable-yards and gateways; every servant in the house jostled and trod on the heels of his fellow; dinner tables were laid in all the parlours; sand, in preparation for the scuffle, was spread on the floor instead of carpets; the lawyers ran to and fro in their wigs, and a group of hungry farmers in the passage, all panting and eager for the fray, whetted their large teeth, and licked their lips, as they snuffed up the sweet savour, or fragrant odour, from the kitchen.

(Sir G. Head, *A Home Tour through the Manufacturing Districts of England in the Summer of 1835*, 2nd edition, 1968, 429)

**1849 Anne Porter**

I reached Lancaster about 5 o'clock – took up our quarters to dine & sleep at the *King's Arms Hotel* – before dinner we walked round the Castle yard …

(Worcester Record Office, BA 3940/66 (i))

**1857 Frances Sayer**

… Reached Lancaster about 2 o'clock. Having looked at our bedrooms, 3 small rooms at the top of the *King's Arms Hotel*, we went out. – there was a drizzling rain during the greater part of the day … Our sitting room was a large uncomfortable looking room with an immense bow window. The dinner was not bad, but altogether we were very glad to have left Lancaster at 10.30 …

(East Sussex County Record Office, SAY 3403)

# Soldiers

Until the Cardwell army reforms of the 1880s which made most regiments territorial in nature, with a fixed recruiting area and fixed barracks, most soldiers had experienced a wandering life. When not on campaign or abroad most were billeted on houses or inns.

In 1813 the Borough Court Rule Book (Rule Book 1784–1822, 118) lists the property of Richard Hamer and the contents of 14 named rooms in his inn (unfortunately not identified) including a bar and the 'Soldiers Barwick' (barracks).

In the 1841 Census Enumerators' Returns we can identify two inns in Penny Street housing soldiers. At the house of William Moore were the following; John Beadman, 30, John Smethurst, 30, Joseph Bentham, 25, and Emmanuel Eckersley, 20, all 'soldiers in Yeomanry'. Nearby at the house of Joseph Sly, perhaps at this date the *Victoria Inn*, were John Ashburner, 39, Thomas Pownall, 44 (a Scot), George Greenhalgh, 35, and William Philtman, 30, again all Yeomanry. Presumably as Yeomanry they were all cavalry and the inns also stabled their horses.

# Coaching inns

The description 'coaching inn' is much loved by the brewers and their publicists. The idea conjures up gleaming brass, coach lamps, horns and other bogus paraphernalia, and the concept itself is usually bogus. True coaching inns were those where the network of coaches met and exchanged or deposited their passengers. They had to be of a certain size, and usually had a yard and large amounts of stabling.

You would book the coach from an inn, eat at inns on your journey, and probably stay at an inn at your destination. You might also change coach there, and certainly there would be brief stops at intermediate inns on the way to change horses. Innkeepers could do well out of the coach traffic and were often joint promoters of the coaches which called at their inns. Traditionally such inns had a yard into which the coach could drive, adequate stabling for the many changes of horses, and facilities for feeding many guests at the same time. They tended to be the larger inns in a town. Many of them also hired out post-chaises, the equivalent of modern taxis, for a more localised market.

In Lancaster the earliest principal inn was the *George* in Market Street, mentioned by a number of seventeenth-century travellers, but already by 1722 it was described as 'a tenement formerly the George Inn'. There were others such as the *King's Arms*, *Sun* and the *Royal Oak*, later joined by the *Commercial Inn* in the Market Place. The *Sun* was the setting-off point for the oversands coach, which ran to Ulverston via the Kent and Leven Sands of Morecambe Bay. It occupied part of a large courtyard building, possibly medieval in date, which belonged to the Molyneux family of south-west Lancashire, but was rebuilt in its present form in 1785.

Coaches seem romantic, with their immaculate turn-out and their hint of speed and foreign places, but they were relatively expensive and served a very small percentage of the population. When the railways came they were driven off the main roads and tended only to survive where they could serve as feeders to the trains, until even that market disappeared. In the last days of coaching the **Old Sir Simon's Inn** in Lancaster became the main point of departure for coaches. Canon Grenside, arriving in December 1846 to take up a curacy at Claughton, remembered seeing the masons finishing work on the Castle Station, ready for its opening, and the two big destination boards outside the **Old Sir Simon's**, showing where the coaches went. (Library, Obituaries Scrapbook, obituary 1916)

It was a time of great change.

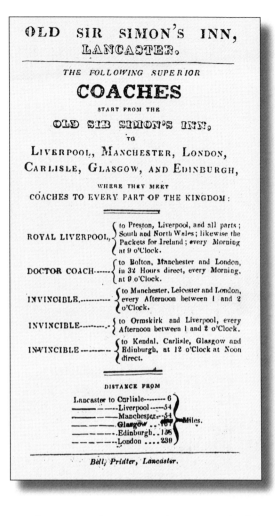

Handbill for coaches leaving the *Old Sir Simon's Inn* in Market Street in 1837. (Lancaster Library)

Inn bills issued by Thexton at the *White Cross and Packet Boat Tavern*, Penny Street, in the late 1830s or 1840s, Joseph Ladyman at the *King's Arms*, 1830, and Henry Calvert at the *Old Sir Simon's Inn* in 1829 and in 1837. (Lancaster Library)

In addition to the coaches many inns also provided post-chaises, light vehicles equivalent to taxis, which could be privately hired and would take the traveller the rest of the way home from the main coaching inns. These appear in many handbills and are evident also in the Rule Books of the Borough Court. When the goods of Matthew Reynolds of the *New Inn* were listed in 1787 they included 3 post-chaises (Rule Book 1784–1822, 9–12) while Robert Bradley had 4 post-chaises among his inn possessions in 1801 (Rule Book 1784–1822, 47). Later on, after the arrival of the railways, the *King's Arms* had its own horse-bus to fetch passengers from the railway station.

The reliance placed upon horses meant that coaching inns required large amounts of stabling, for the change of horses required at each stage. The tired and sweating horses needed to be fed, rubbed down and quickly placed in warm stabling if they were to remain in peak condition. This in turn meant that experienced ostlers and stable-lads were required to look after them. The arrival of a coach in the inn yard would lead to a great deal of bustle as the passengers descended, perhaps for a meal, while the driver and guard checked the coach over. The tired horses were led away to the stables while fresh ones were brought out and harnessed. Then the luggage of new passengers was hoisted on to the roof and into the basket at the back, the passengers reassembled, and off the coach would go again. The smartness of the turn-out and the punctuality of timing were important features. In the halcyon days of coaching, in the period 1810–30, the drivers of the principal coaches were regarded as heroes, and dressed the part in immaculate trousers and boots, and with fashionable greatcoats over all, with many capes against the rain and cold. Young bloods sought to emulate them, and might be allowed temporary control of the reins as a great favour.

At the top of the tree was the Mail, its coaches beautifully turned out, its horses of the best, and its timekeeping immaculate. Being on the main west-coast road Lancaster had several mailcoaches passing through. By the 1840s this chapter was over, the railways triumphant, and many people prophesied that roads would pass out of use forever. The railways themselves fostered hotels near their stations and such business compensated a little for the loss of coaching inns.

## Market Houses

Some inns did good business on market days, when farmers came into Lancaster from the countryside around. They needed stabling for their horses, somewhere to park a cart if they had brought one, somewhere for a drink to seal a bargain, and somewhere to eat. Town-centre inns could offer all these things, and on such days every room, including those normally let to travellers, would be pressed into service as places to eat.

View of the Market Place *c.*1765 by an anonymous artist. This shows the old Town Hall of 1671 to the left, but three inns as well. In the centre is the ***Royal Oak*** with the name of its landlord, Wm Sharp, over the door. Next to it is the ***George & Dragon***. Finally, to the right is the ***Blue Anchor***, still recognisable after more than two hundred and forty years. Between the ***Royal Oak*** and the Town Hall is Mr Hornby's Great House, later to become the site of the ***Commercial Inn***. (Whitworth Art Gallery, Manchester)

Sir George Head's description of his arrival in Lancaster in 1835 (see p. 3) gives a vivid view of one such occasion, in this case the Assizes, when the same conditions prevailed. Thomas Gray had the misfortune of arriving on fair day, with similar consequences.

Stabling was usually at the rear of the inn, and in most cases has now disappeared in favour of garages or other buildings. Its quality and quantity was crucial to the success of an inn, and one or more ostlers would be kept to take care of the horses left there. Charges for feed etc. when horses were stabled overnight might equal the cost of a traveller's meals.

The principal feature of such inns was 'the ordinary', usually manifesting itself as a long table or tables where all guests sat together, in no particular order, and ate a set series of dishes provided by the inn. This made cooking a great deal easier, as it did not involve individual choices and short orders. In 1843 E. Lofthouse advertised that he would serve up an excellent dinner for farmers every Saturday at half past twelve at the *Sun Inn*. (*Lancaster Gazette*, 3/6/1843)

In the eighteenth and nineteenth centuries many more people were employed upon the land, and most farms were very small by today's standards. Conversely there were many more individual farmers, with more diverse farming practises, who had business to contract on market days, with stock to buy and sell, dairy products such as butter and cheese – there were specific cheese fairs in Lancaster – and corn to sell at the corn exchange. Such people would also take the opportunity to look up friends, conduct legal business, and buy provisions. Hence the inns which served as market houses did good business.

There were also hiring fairs for servants which took place twice a year, in spring and autumn, in the days when most farm servants lived in, and moved on regularly from farm to farm on six-monthly contracts, as was the northern custom. On hiring days the streets were full of men and women carrying some token of their trade, and the inns were full of farmers and successful servants who had been hired, celebrating their bargain with a drink. It was an opportunity for a brief holiday from a hard life and many entertainments and sideshows were put on at this time. Later on in the nineteenth century, hiring fairs were replaced by longer contracts and by agencies which made arrangements, instead of the *ad hoc* street fairs.

## Brewing

Brewing lay at the very heart of innkeeping for many centuries. Inns and beerhouses usually served beer brewed on the premises until the mid to late nineteenth century. The quality of the beer was one of the distinguishing features of an inn, at a time when there were no well-known national brands. Until this point larger brewers had been rare outside London. A new breed of large brewers which owned a string of inns and obliged their tenants to serve their beer began to be established at this time. Home brewing had accounted for roughly half of all British beer

Brewing, from W. H. Pyne's *Microcosm* of 1808, Plate XIII.

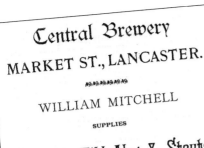

Central Brewery
MARKET ST., LANCASTER.

WILLIAM MITCHELL

SUPPLIES

Bitter & Mild Ales & Stouts

ON THE MOST REASONABLE TERMS
IN LARGE OR SMALL QUANTITIES

ALES

| | | | |
|---|---|---|---|
| X Mild, Small Barrels | ... | ... | 1/2 per gallon |
| Ditto 18 gallons | 20/- | | |
| XX Mild, Small Barrels | ... | ... | 1/4 per gallon |
| Ditto 18 gallons | 23/- | | |
| XXX Mild, Small Barrels | ... | ... | 1/7 per gallon |
| Ditto 18 gallons | 26/- | | |
| Bitter Ales and Stouts 1/4 per gallon | | | |

MINERAL WATER MANUFACTURER.

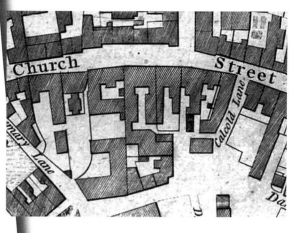

*Left:* Advertisement for Mitchell's Central Brewery in 1889. This brewery stood behind the **New Inn**, off Market Street, and its site is now partly marked by The Vue multiplex cinema.

*Above:* Detail from Mackreth's map of 1778 showing Calcold (*recte* Calkeld) Lane. The third building to the left of the lane is the **White Hart**, before North Road was cut through. In its yard was a very good water supply for brewing, perhaps even the 'Cold Well' after which the lane was named by Norse-speaking settlers.

in 1801, a figure which had fallen to practically nil by a century later. In Lancaster two larger brewers were established by the late nineteenth century, Yates & Jackson and Mitchells.

That is not to say that there had not been specialist brewers who supplied various inns, perhaps helped by a particular reputation or a good source of water. As far back as 1778 Lancaster had a specialist brewery, shown on Mackreth's map next to Brewery Lane, off Moor Lane. Known as the 'Old Brewery' this was occupied in 1853 by Mr Sly, publican of the *Royal Oak* in Market Square, who advertised his 'October Ales' in the *Lancaster Guardian* (*Lancaster Guardian*, 12/11/1853). This brewery was on the same site as that later used by Yates & Jackson, and later still by Mitchell's, so its position may well have been dictated by a good water supply. A date stone on the outside of this (now disused) brewery gives the date 1669, which may indicate that is goes even further back, but there is no documentary evidence as early as this. Another large brewery detached from any inn stood in the late nineteenth century between Brock Street and Lucy Street. It was known as the Brock Street Brewery and was built in 1881 and operated by Mr F. Cornforth in 1889. It is marked on the very large scale (1:500) Ordnance Survey of 1892. Yates & Jackson also had premises in this vicinity.

However, it is clear that most Lancaster inns brewed their own beer prior to the late nineteenth century. The Rule Books of the Borough Court are full of references to public houses and most of them list brewing vessels in the Cellar or the Brew House. A skilled brewer was important, but the quality of water was equally so. A spring in Calkeld Lane, behind the former *White Hart*, was long famous for the quality of its water for brewing. A very few inns show no evidence at all for brewing. Some of these instead list extensive wine cellars, so there may have been a divide between the inns catering for travellers (wine and port) and those serving a local community (beer). The Act of 1830 which established beerhouses was designed to encourage beer-drinking at the expense of spirits, especially gin.

Two examples from probate inventories show brewhouses and stocks of ale and wine:

---

Elizabeth Skirrow of Lancaster 1731 [*Bear & Staff*] (LRO WRW/A 1731)

**Brew House**

| | |
|---|---|
| A large copper for brewing in, a small ditto, a malt mill & iron grates | 7–0–0 |
| 2 mash knops, 2 working knops, & 4 barrells & 2 water-gallons & 2 hogsheads | 0–19–0 |

**Cellar**

| | |
|---|---|
| 175 Gallons of ale at 12d per gallon | 8–15–0 |

Robert Borranskill of Lancaster 1726 [*Mermaid*] (LRO WRW/A 1726)

**Brewhouse**

| | |
|---|---|
| A large brewing pan, 1 iron boiler, 10 brewing vessels | 5–5–0 |

**Ale cellar**

| | |
|---|---|
| Ale | 5–0–0 |
| Hogs heads and barrells | 1–16–0 |
| In the other ale cellar 7 hogsheads, 1 table, 1 pipe 1 bottle creel | 1–0–0 |

**Wine cellar**

| | |
|---|---|
| 1 hogshead & half & some small casks of wine, 3 empty hogsheads, 2 halfs 4 barrells | 25–0–0 |

---

Until the late eighteenth century beer was the standard drink at mealtimes. Tea and coffee had been fashionable for some time, but initially their cost had put them out of reach of ordinary people. Now they started to become more common, but 'small' (weak) beer was still very popular as an everyday drink, and many people still brewed at home, especially in the country.

Brewing consisted of six main processes. Barley was the usual source of beer. The first stage, malting the barley, was specialised and might be carried out elsewhere, the finished malt being bought in. Yates & Jackson began in the early 1870s as Jackson & Yates, Maltsters. The process involved heating and turning the grain on a special floor to stop it sprouting, and to impart flavour. Then came mashing, boiling, cooling, fermentation and finally racking. Mashing released sugars from the malt and water. These became the 'wort', the liquor for fermentation, which was then boiled with hops to add flavour. The wort was next run off into tubs or trays and allowed to cool. Then it was put into the fermenting tun with yeast, which gradually turned the sugars into alcohol. The final process involved removing the debris of fermentation and clarifying the brew, which was run off into casks. The malt grains left behind after the first mashing process might be used again, up to three times, each time

Programme for Lifeboat Saturday, August 1, 1903, including advertisements for the *Mitre Inn* and the *Queens Commercial Hotel* (Whittle Springs Celebrated Ales).

producing a weaker brew at the end. This weak brew was the so-called 'small beer', for table use. Brewing varied in scale, but used these same basic processes.

Transport improvements, especially the coming of the railways, improved the prospects for large brewers. The water of Burton-on-Trent, with its natural gypsum content, produced very superior light sparkling ales, which had a national sale once transport speeded up. London breweries already had the advantage of scale and capital, but until beer would travel safely and without losing its flavour it had little impact on the north. Improvements in bottling also led to an increase in off-licence sales, either through existing inns or through specialist shops which began to penetrate the suburbs. Much beer was sold by the jug at the side doors of inns, but this trade was much disliked by magistrates, because it was often children who were sent to fetch it.

The Whittle Springs Brewery, at Whittle near Chorley, seems to have captured some of the local market. In 1903 the **Queen's Commercial Hotel** in Penny Street was advertising 'Whittle Springs Celebrated Ales', while so marked was the connection with the **Golden Lion** in Moor Lane that it is still sometimes referred to as the '**Whittle Springs**'.

The two local brewers emerged in the latter part of the nineteenth century. Yates & Jackson had their brewery in Moor Lane and Brewery Lane, and came to own many local inns. William Mitchell, himself a former publican who began at the **Black Horse** in 1871, built his brewery in the town centre, between Church Street and Market Street and right behind the **New Inn**, which was supplied with beer directly. Yates & Jackson were the first to go, in 1985, selling out their interests to Thwaites of Blackburn. Soon, Mitchells were persuaded to take over their former brewery as it had a better water supply and this would also free up a town centre site, with difficult access for transport, for development. They moved out in 1988. It was quite a shock, locally, when Mitchells themselves moved out of brewing in 1999. They still continue as owners of a chain of pubs, currently totalling fourteen in Lancaster alone.

From the nineteenth century onwards a number of other brewers had owned or supplied pubs in Lancaster, some of them operating on a national scale such as Watneys, Bass or Courage, and others more regional such as Vaux, Scottish & Newcastle, Boddingtons, Jennings or Thwaites. Choice is now much greater, and tied houses such as these will probably diminish, especially as beer becomes less significant as a proportion of sales. Small-scale brewing has also returned in recent years, with the appearance of so-called micro-breweries, and in 2009 there were two of these serving the Lancaster area, but what the long-term future may be is at present unknown, especially when the micro-brewery is sustained only by the enthusiasm and hard work of individuals, and may not outlast them.

# Food

We tend to think of pub food as a modern concept, but in fact it goes right back to the earliest days and was always as important as drink, both to travellers and landlords. Probably it was the rise of small town-centre pubs and beerhouses in the nineteenth century which brought us the drink-only premises, largely as a result of there being too little room. The inn kitchen was a large and well-equipped place where the poorer travellers or servants might lodge and sleep. It had the advantage of being the warmest part of the inn.

Farmers' ordinaries, meals for coach-travellers and food for groups and societies which met there were important preoccupations for the landlord. Many also went beyond their premises to provide public dinners, perhaps because they had the kitchens, serving dishes and cutlery to do so. Jane Noon of the *Royal Oak* was famous for her external catering.

We have already seen William Monson's comments on the Lancashire custom of loading the table with all sorts of extra food beyond that which was ordered, which he met with in 1816 at the *King's Arms*. Some inns offered speciality dishes. The *King's Arms* offered bridecake as its speciality when Charles Dickens visited in 1857.

> '... good old inn, established in a good old house, an inn where they give you bridecake every day after dinner ...'
>
> (Cross-Fleury, *Time-Honoured Lancaster*, 1891, 451)

## ROYAL-OAK INN,

### MARKET-PLACE, LANCASTER.

—⚬⚬⚬⚬—

## *JANE NOON,*

GRATEFUL to her Friends, for the Encouragement fhe has met with in Bufinefs, refpectfully informs the Ladies, Gentlemen, Travellers, and others, that a large and convenient AD-DITION has recently been made to the above old-eftablifhed INN, which, with its advantage-ous Situation, renders it particularly well calculated for the accommodation of Travellers, having a great Number of SINGLE BED-ROOMS, SITTING-ROOMS, &c. now finifhed and neatly fitted up for the Reception of her Friends; and by always keeping a Stock of the beft WINES and LIQUORS, with affiduous Attention of herfelf and Servants, fhe hopes to merit that Approbation and Patronage, which it will ever be her utmoft Study to deferve.

\*\*\* NEW and EXCELLENT STABLING, with a CAREFUL OSTLER.

January 15th, 1803.

The Mayor held an annual Venison Feast at the *Bear & Staff* until 1803.

Apart from the 'ordinary', held on market and other special days, one thing which we should find strange was the custom in the eighteenth and early nineteenth century of serving food in many different rooms within an inn. This was probably due to the lack of space for a single restaurant. It meant that bedrooms were often dragooned into use as eating rooms, with tables and chairs drawn up as required. It serves to explain the wide variety of furniture recorded in bedrooms in inventories and the Rule Books.

The serving of food has once more become significant business for urban inns, offering a better profit margin for landlords than the drink which they often have to buy and sell at prices set high by the brewers or owners. The wheel has gone full circle as food customers have become more important than drinkers.

*Opposite:* Advertisement for the *Royal Oak*, Market Place, proprietor Jane Noon, who had just taken it over in 1803. (CRO Barrow-in-Furness, Soulby Coll.)

*Left:* Inn bill issued by William Pilling at the *Nag's Head*, Church Street, between 1822 and 1829.

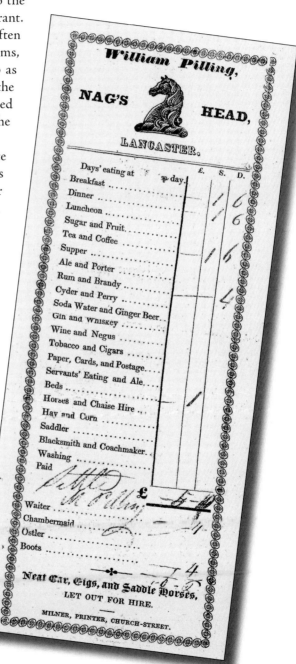

## Auctions and Sales

Until the late nineteenth century, when specialised sale-rooms were established, it was normal for land, buildings and goods to be auctioned in inns. There are many advertisements for such auctions in local newspapers and on handbills. Inns could provide the necessary space for interested parties, while they made their profits on serving food and drink to both bidders and auctioneers. Larger inns did the most business in this line, especially the *King's Arms* in Market Street, which as the premier inn had a head start on others.

One person much involved in this business was William Stewardson, who between 1876 and 1877 kept a notebook of his commercial affairs. He was a busy man – auctioneer, paper-hanger, painter and gilder and house and land agent. Most of his business was concerned with valuations, however. He records many sales in Lancaster and the villages around, and many of his valuations were for subsequent sales. He valued the contents of the *White Lion* in St Leonardgate, *St George's Tavern*, the *Bay Horse*, China Lane, and the *Fleece Inn*, Penny Street, all over a space of a couple of months. Inns were also sold at inns, as was the case of the *Spink Bull* in China Lane, sold at the *Cross Keys* in Market Street. His valuations in the area around included the *Carnforth Inn* in 1877 and the *Shakespeare Teetotal Inn* at Melling in 1876. (MS valuation book 1876–77, City Museum, LM99.1)

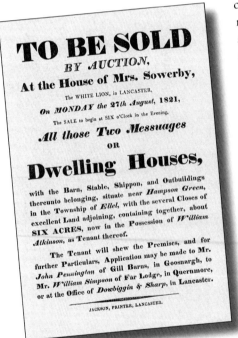

Sale of houses at the *White Lion*, Mrs Sowerby, 1821. (Lancaster Library)

Probably very much more was sold by auction in the eighteenth and nineteenth centuries than is today. Farming land and stock was traditionally sold this way, and still is, as the countryside has a marked preference for auctions over fixed price sales. Anything of which the potential value is uncertain may be sold by auction. Probably the main cause of the popularity of auction, though, was the absence of alternative methods. Some firms of solicitors acted in private treaty sales, or as go-betweens, but not until the late nineteenth century were there estate agents and other middlemen with windows to advertise goods and land, so most was displayed on handbills or in the newspapers. The whole thing was regarded as a good day out, with excitement, a chance to insert one's nose into a neighbour's affairs, and food and drink.

## TO BE SOLD

BY AUCTION,

At the House of the late Mrs. ELLEN GOTH,

KNOWN BY THE SIGN OF THE SHIP,

In Damside Street, Lancaster,

On MONDAY the 5th day of NOVEMBER, 1827,

AT SIX O'CLOCK in the Evening;

ALL THAT

## MESSUAGE
OR
### Dwelling House,

NOW USED AS A

## PUBLIC HOUSE,

AND KNOWN BY THE SIGN OF THE

## SHIP,

SITUATE IN DAMSIDE STREET, IN LANCASTER,

Late in the possession of the said Mrs. ELLEN GOTH.

ALSO, ALL THOSE FIVE

### Messuages or Dwelling Houses,

Adjoining the said last mentioned Dwelling House, Now in the several possessions of Thomas Hodgson, Thomas Hudleston, Edward Barrow, John Askew and Richard Mason, as Tenants.

ALSO, ALL THAT OTHER

*Messuage or Dwelling House,*

Situate in St. Leonard Gate, in Lancaster aforesaid, now in the possession of Mrs. Briggs, as Tenant.

*The above Premises are all in excellent Repair, and are of Freehold Tenure.*

The respective Tenants will shew the same, and for further Particulars apply to Mr. WILLAN, Solicitor, Church Street, Lancaster. *Lancaster, October 15th, 1827.*

JACKSON, PRINTER, LANCASTER.

---

The Creditors of the late Mrs. HANNAH WILSON, of the Commercial Inn, in Lancaster, deceased, are desired to meet the Executors named in her Will, on *Friday the 19th October,* 1821, at the Commercial Inn, at 4 o'Clock in the Afternoon, in order to give Directions as to the arrangement and disposal of the Estate and Effects of the said *Hannah Wilson.*

Lancaster, 9th October, 1821.

Jackson, Printer, New-street, Lancaster.

---

Group of advertisements for sales at the *Ship Inn, King's Arms, Green Dragon, New Inn, Bear & Staff,* and *White Lion,* and for a creditors' meeting at the *Commercial Inn.* (Lancaster Library)

---

## TO BE SOLD

BY AUCTION,

At the House of Mr. JOHN PRITT,

The King's Arms Inn, in Lancaster,

IN THE COUNTY OF LANCASTER,

On Monday the 12th Day of January, 1824,

The Sale to begin at Six o'Clock in the Evening;

(Subject to such Conditions as will then and there be produced,)

ALL THAT

## MESSUAGE
OR
## Dwelling House

With the Yard, Buildings, and Appurtenances thereunto belonging, called and known by the Name or Sign of the

### Boot and Shoe,

Situate in the Market-Street, near the Horse-Shoe-Corner, in Lancaster aforesaid, in the Possession of Mr. Wm. Newton, as Tenant thereof.

ALSO, ALL THAT

### Seat or Pew,

No. 133, situate and being in the South Gallery of the Chapel of Saint Ann, in Lancaster aforesaid, now in the Possession of Mr. George Carruthers, as Tenant thereof.

Mr. ANTHONY BATESON PROCTER, of Lancaster aforesaid, will shew the Premises, and further Particulars may be had by Application at the Office of Mr. SHARP, Solicitor, in Lancaster.

Lancaster, 26th December, 1823.

SILL, PRINTER, LANCASTER.

---

## TO BE SOLD,

By Auction,

On MONDAY the 14th Day of SEPTEMBER, 1795,

At the HOUSE of JOHN GARTH,

The Sign of the NEW INN in Lancaster, in the County of Lancaster,

The Sale to begin at 7 o'Clock in the Evening.

ALL that the said commodious well known and established Messuage or Dwellinghouse and Inn, situate in and fronting to the Market Street in Lancaster aforesaid,

CALLED

## THE NEW INN,

with the Yard, Stables, Barns, Coach Houses and Buildings, occupied therewith, now in the Possession of the said John Garth.

AND ALSO all that Messuage or Dwelling-house and two Shops adjoining the said Inn, and fronting to Market Street aforesaid, with the Counting House and Warehouse, (now converted into and used as a Tallow Chandler's Shop) and Vaults behind and under the said Dwelling-house, AND ALSO all that Cooper's Shop and Stable near thereto, now in the several Possessions of the said John Garth, and of Robert Hudson, Robert Parkinson, Thomas Noon, John Procter, Robert Simpson and Henry Couart.

The respective Tenants will shew the Premises and further Particulars may be had by applying to Mr. Isaac Capstick, of Caton near Lancaster or at the Office of Mr. Baldwin, Attorney at Law in Lancaster.

A. BUSHER, PRINTER.

---

## To be Let,

BY TICKET,

At the House of Thomas Camm,

The GREEN DRAGON, in LANCASTER,

On FRIDAY the 22d Day of September, 1815,

At SIX o'Clock in the Evening;

All that very eligible Farm,

KNOWN BY THE NAME OF

## Lingart,

Situate near to the Market Town of Garstang, consisting of a Messuage, Barns and Outbuildings, Orchard, Garden, and of 64A. 1R. 11P. more or less, of very fertile Lands, late in the Possession of William Parkinson, as Tenant thereof.

And also, an Allotment,

On BARNACRE MOOR, containing 7A. 3R. 32P.

Also, all that TENEMENT and FARM,

KNOWN BY THE NAME OF

## Starbank and Bondgate,

Situate in Ellel, in the County of Lancaster, containing 103A. 2R. 2P. Customary Measure, of seven Yards.

Further Particulars may be known by application to JOHN FENTON CAWTHORNE, Esquire, the Owner; or at the Office of Messrs. Dowbiggin, Sharp and Rawlinson, Solicitors, in Lancaster.

JACKSON, P...

---

## TO BE LET,

At the House of Mr. WILLIAM RIPPON,

THE BEAR AND STAFF, IN LANCASTER,

On SATURDAY the 31st Day of MAY, 1817,

At SIX o'Clock in the Evening;

ALL THE GREAT AND SMALL

## TITHES,

IN LOWER WYERSDALE,

Belonging to the Rev. JAMES THOMAS of Lancaster, and JAMES BOURNE, Esq. of Liverpool; now farmed by Mr. RICHARD JENKINSON, of Lower Wyersdale.

Further Particulars may be known, by Application at the Office of Messrs. DOWBIGGIN and SHARP, in Lancaster.

JACKSON, Printer, Lancaster.

---

## TO BE SOLD

BY AUCTION,

AT MRS. POWELL'S, THE WHITE LION INN,

IN LANCASTER,

On Monday, the 16th Day of October, 1837,

The Sale to begin at Four o'Clock in the Afternoon,

A VERY DESIRABLE

## TITHE-FREE
## ESTATE,

Situate in Littledale,

# Carriers

Because of their central positions and their long hours of business many town inns found themselves involved in the carrying business. Rarely did the landlords themselves operate as carriers, but the inns formed excellent starting points and had room to gather parcels and other goods in readiness. There was, until the later nineteenth century, no parcel post, so that any goods which needed to be forwarded elsewhere either had to be taken by friends or relations in their personal luggage, or sent by road coach, which was expensive. Carriers offered a cheap and reliable alternative, especially for the local area. Valuable and perishable goods such as food or game might travel in the boot of a coach, as speed was often of the essence. Less valuable or perishable goods could afford to take longer on the road, if the cost was less.

There were two sorts of carrier. The first operated the long-distance waggons, pulled by many horses and progressing at a stately 2 to 3 miles per hour. Concern about the damage to road surfaces meant that laws were enacted controlling the width of wheels, and these waggons often as a result had very wide wheels to spread the load. They also acted as the poor person's coach, offering a modicum of shelter and protection as well as company, even if the traveller chose to walk beside them with the waggoner. In 1794 you could send your goods to London via the waggon which left the *Old Sir Simon's* every Monday and Thursday. Its destination was the *Castle Inn* in Wood Street, London. (*Universal British Directory*, 1794) A waggon returned every Tuesday and Friday to the *Old Sir Simon's*. Each waggon would have taken some five or six days to do the journey of 240 miles. In 1811 John Hargreaves advertised that he was taking on the carrying concern formerly run by a partnership of himself and his wife Ann, and Messrs. Welsh & Poulson. (*Lancaster Gazette* 26/10/1811) His waggons would set out every day (Sundays excepted) from his warehouses in Bridge Street, Manchester, calling at

Page from Baines' Directory of 1825, showing the carriers then departing from the various Lancaster inns.

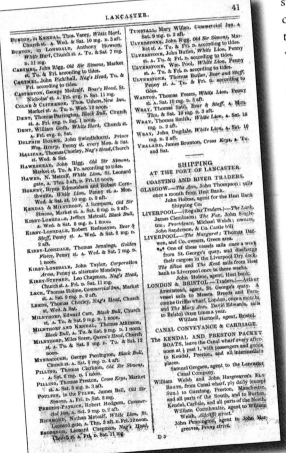

Preston, Lancaster, Kendal, Penrith, Carlisle, Glasgow and Edinburgh. His local contact in Lancaster was Thomas Parkinson, perhaps the landlord of that name who kept the **Crooked Billet.**

At the other end of the scale was the multitude of local carriers, usually based in the villages around each town. They provided the basic local network of contacts and no doubt carried news and rumour as well as goods. In the late eighteenth or early nineteenth century they adopted light two-wheel spring-carts with canvas tilts for protection, which were reasonably fast compared with the waggons. An advert by Robert Atkinson junior in 1811 is quite instructive. (*Lancaster Gazette*, 23/2/1811) He had commenced carrying goods between Lancaster, Burton and Kendal. He would be at Lancaster on Monday and Friday and at Kendal on Wednesday and Saturday. Goods left at the **White Lion**, Lancaster, the **King's Arms**, Burton, and the **New Inn**, Kendal, would be carefully forwarded with all speed. He lived at Holme, near Burton.

According to Baines' Directory of 1825 some forty carriers, including two women (they may have been proprietors, employing others to do the work), set out from Lancaster every week and sometimes several times each week for destinations as close as Wray, Hornby or Pilling, or as far afield as Halifax, Richmond or over the sands to Cartmel, Ulverston or Hawkshead. Thirty years later, in 1855, one of these men, John Rigg, was still covering the same route to Cartmel and Ulverston over the sands every Tuesday and Friday from the **Old Sir Simon's**, at times depending upon the tides. Almost certainly the opening of the Furness Railway around Morecambe Bay in 1857 will have seen him off. By 1881 no carriers are listed crossing the sands to Furness, but in that year some forty-five different carriers, including two women, were still setting off for thirty-three different destinations.

In 1835 Thomas and John Bentham advertised themselves as carriers to and from Lancaster, Bentham, Settle, Leeds, and other parts of Yorkshire, having succeeded Leonard Sedgwick as carriers to and from the same places. They would arrive at the **White Hart** Inn, Lancaster, every Tuesday and Friday, and return to Bentham on the following days, and at the **Naked Man**, Settle, every Monday and Thursday, and return to Bentham on the same days. Thus they operated a double network and, via Settle, a link with the manufacturing district round Leeds. (*Lancaster Gazette*, 13/6/1835)

The inns named made good gathering-points for packages, and everyone knew where to find them. There were no doubt many regular customers such as tradesmen who used them for both raw materials and finished goods, while produce such as garden stuff could be sent via the carrier from the gardens of country houses to their owners' town houses.

It is probable that the last carriers were operating as late as the 1930s, by which time cheap motor vans were reasonably common. These people were at the very end of a long tradition going back some three centuries, in which carts set off on regular journeys on specific days from specific inn-yards, serving villages and farms on their route. Many of the carriers took messages or ran small errands for their older and more housebound customers. It seems to be a system worth reinventing.

# Elections

At Parliamentary election time the inns really came into their own. Both sides used them shamelessly for bribing the electorate, and a considerable sum fell into the hands of the landlords where 'treating' took place. The (entirely male) electorate was invited into certain inns for food, drink or actual cash bribes in return for their vote. The open hustings and lack of a secret ballot encouraged such things. Here is a list of inns in Lancaster used for 'treating' at the election by Sir Thomas Egerton in 1772, in the John Rylands Library, Manchester:

| | | | |
|---|---|---|---|
| William Bentham | *Barley Mow* | Hugh Ravencroft | *[ ]* |
| John Stevenson | *Naggs Head* | James Leech | *White Hart* |
| William Howson | *Bear & Staff* | John Batson | *Wheatsheaf* |
| Henry Whiteside | *Ship* | Richard Walton | *Green Man* |
| Anthony Blezard | *Horse & Farrier* | Richard Crosfield | *Queens Head* |
| James Vicars | *Bulls Head* | John Parkinson | *White Lion* |
| John Capstick | *New Inn* | Thomas Spence | *Plaisterers Arms* |
| John Royle | *Royal Oak* | James Bland | *Green Dragon* |
| Joseph Norman | *Sun* | Mr. Reynolds | *Kings Arms* |
| Simeon Dodgson | *Boot & Shoe* | Henry Whiteside | *Cross Keys* |
| Robert Bannister | *Green Hare* [sic] | | |
| Margaret Crozer | *Sir Simons* | (John Rylands Library, Ryl. Eng. MS 470) | |

The treating cost Egerton over £3,400, a staggering amount for a smallish town in the late eighteenth century. Even then this list is by no means a complete list of all inns in Lancaster at the time, presumably as the opposition candidate was also treating, in other inns!

As well as providing opportunities for bribery, the inns hired by each party were used as committee rooms. It was here that other actions were planned, including breaking windows in houses known to belong to the opposition, and stockpiling eggs for throwing at the hustings or at the chairing of members, often a bloody and brutal affair, leading to considerable violence. William Hogarth's famous sequence of four election cartoons satirises the riotous Oxfordshire elections of 1754 and it is probable that this was also typical in most places. (S.Shesgreen (ed.), *Engravings by Hogarth*, 1973, 86–9) Despite reforms intended to widen the basis of the electorate and to remove the worst abuses of the system in 1832 and after, the habit of 'treating' seems to have continued unabated, especially in the old boroughs where the electorate was based upon freemen, and thus quite small.

At the Lancaster election of 1865, the subject of 'treating' in inns formed the core of a complaint by the losing Tory candidate, leading to a Royal Commission. The evidence was later published in several forms (see Sources). Here some forty inns and beerhouses were systematically approached by the Liberal organisers and paid substantial sums for room hire and drink, while local 'sub-captains', each responsible for a few streets, gathered voters and led them into one of the inns where they would be fed, given drinks (brandy was the preference, apparently, people's taste rising to the opportunities for free liquor) and cash bribes for their vote, if necessary.

Bribing the electorate was costly, but not quite as costly as one might imagine, as the vote was only held by quite a small body of freemen and property-owners. The beerhouses cost the Liberals £3–£5 each, while inns came in dearer at £7 10s. – £15. One inn, *Old Sir Simon's*, was turned down because its licensee wanted £20. Meanwhile the Tories were doing the same in other inns and beerhouses, such as the *Traveller's Rest* in Penny Street. Of course such open corruption was widespread, but usually both sides sought to brush it under the carpet and were not anxious to bring in officialdom. In Lancaster, however, the Tories were so angry at losing that they made an issue of it, resulting in the loss of parliamentary representation for the next twenty years.

Similar events occurred in 1896, when complaints were investigated following the election in 1895 of Col. Foster of Hornby Castle, for the Conservatives. Similar allegations were made, but not this time substantiated. It was said that blue cards were handed out to potential voters, presumably to exchange for drink or food. This time a number of detectives were watching, although not, apparently, to any great purpose.

Subsequently the widening of the electorate and the secret ballot rendered 'treating' superfluous, although the tradition continues in a mild way with party activists offering lifts to the polling station to uncommitted voters. However, we now see no abuse as open and gross as these eighteenth- and nineteenth-century examples, although postal balloting seems to be offering some opportunities. No longer do the inns play a key role.

Detail from one of Hogarth's election cartoons, 1754. The roistering and drinking was probably generally applicable to any borough election at the time.

NOTICE TO

# Creditors.

WHEREAS *RICHARD NUTTALL*, of Skerton, in the County of Lancaster, Victualler, hath this Day assigned over ALL his Estate and Effects, unto Trustees, for an equal Distribution amongst all his Creditors, without any preference.

The Creditors of the said *Richard Nuttall*, are requested forthwith to deliver an Account of their respective Demands against him, at the Office of Messrs. *Dowbiggin & Sharp*, in Lancaster.

And all those who stand indebted to the said *Richard Nuttall*, are requested to pay what they severally owe, at the Office of the said *Dowbiggin & Sharp* without Delay, or Proceedings at Law will be taken for the Recovery thereof.

# To be Sold

## BY AUCTION,

*At the House of the said RICHARD NUTTALL,*

At the BLUE ANCHOR, in SKERTON,

On *TUESDAY* the 28th Day of *JANUARY*, 1817,

The SALE to begin at TWELVE o'Clock at NOON:

All his the said RICHARD NUTTALL's

# Household Goods

## *And FURNITURE,*

Consisting of Beds and Bedding, Clock and Case, Mahogany Tables and Chests of Drawers, together with Brewing Vessels and Kitchen Furniture.

*And also, all his the said RICHARD NUTTALL's*

# Stock of CATTLE,

## *HAY, STRAW and PIGS, &c.*

N. B. Time for Payment will be fixed at the Place of Sale.

*JACKSON, Printer, Lancaster.*

Notice to creditors of Richard Nuttall of the *Blue Anchor*, Skerton, 1817. Bankruptcy unfortunately was, and still is, a common occurrence among licensees. Nuttall seems to have also been a farmer, judging by his stock. (Lancaster Library)

# CHAPTER TWO

# Innkeepers

## Who ran the inns?

A GREAT VARIETY OF PEOPLE ran inns in Lancaster. They ranged from whole dynasties brought up in the trade to individuals who spent only a few months or years in it. The employment of some was probably so short-lived that we are not even aware of them, occurring as they may between successive editions of the trade directories. As far as families were concerned it was probably a great bonus to have experienced support from both children and grandparents from time to time, while in the days when many inns brewed their own beer there was no substitute for long practice. We shall see the extensive role of women in running the inns, either as licensees or as supporters.

We can infer an attitude towards a career in innkeeping from the town's Apprentice Rolls of the eighteenth century. Nine innkeepers over that period apprenticed their sons to other trades, but no-one apprenticed their sons to an innkeeper. It seems that either it was a trade that was relatively easy to get into, and to sink or swim as one could, or that innkeepers as a group regarded one of the established trades as less risky or more respectable.

Some innkeepers, clearly careerists, moved from inn to inn. In the 1850s, for which a series of books entitled *Lancaster 50 Years Ago* contain extracts from the local newspapers, we can see the process clearly. At each licensing session a number of licensees move on from inn to inn. A few retire or die, and a few with no previous experience move in. The process seems to have gone on earlier and still goes on today. In 1843 E. Lofthouse and W. Bagot, who had kept the *Sir Simon's* and the *Sun Inn* respectively, changed houses. A case of the grass being greener on the other side of the fence? The two inns were different in character, the *Sir Simon's* being a travellers' inn, while the *Sun* by this time catered mainly for farmers. Thomas Camm ran the *Green Dragon* in 1816, the *Bear & Staff* in 1820–22 (he was declared bankrupt in 1822), the *Fox & Goose* in 1825 and the *Golden Fleece* in 1828. Bankruptcy was a severe risk in the trade. In his diary, David Cragg of Wyresdale recorded three publicans in

Lancaster who failed and sold up in 1822 alone, those at the *Bear & Staff*, the *Green Dragon* and an unnamed house in Market Street. This source is unfortunately somewhat spoiled by faulty transcription. (G. Fandrey (ed.), *The Craggs of Greenbank*, nd but *c*.1974, *sub* 1822) Several others are known from the same year from other sources, such as Martha Sowerby of the *White Lion*. (Rule Book, 1784–1822, 168–70) At the other extreme were those who kept an inn in the family for generations. Jane Noon, herself a third generation female licensee, ran the *Royal Oak* for 36 years from 1803 until 1839. John Goth and his widow Ellen successively ran the *Ship* in Damside Street from at least 1789–1827 (38 years), while John Longfield (unless it was father and son of the same name) ran the *Bird in Hand* in Skerton from at least 1796–1844 (48 years). The *Black Horse* in Common Garden Street seems to have attracted uncommon loyalty, with Agnes Starkie from 1818–1856 (if she was the A. Starkie of 1818) and then William Mitchell from at least 1871–1913, reigns of 38 and 42 years respectively. Margaret Brown took on the *Cross Keys* in 1853, then married William Bullfield in 1858. He took over as licensee until some time after 1871, when he died. Margaret married again, to William Smith, and he duly appears as licensee, but by the 1881 census she was herself the licensee again, as Margaret Smith, William presumably having died in the interim.

At the other end of the spectrum were those whose tenure was extremely brief. Some probably do not even register in the records that survive. Of some 36 innkeepers who left wills in the period between 1748 and 1812 only 16 can be identified with particular inns, partly because of the lack of Trade Directories in that period to tie them down, but partly because the tenure of most was probably very brief. The Election Petition relating to the corrupt election of 1865 gives us an interesting view of a year in which there were no Trade Directories. Many of the names of innkeepers which occur are not those of the Directory of 1864. One John Morland, who was a farmer in 1865, had taken on the *White Horse* in Church Street by 1866. By 1871 he was no longer in the licensed trade. As is the case today, many people whose lifetime ambition is to run an inn find that the reality is not what they expected; either the profits are smaller or the time-commitment is greater. A growing feature during the later nineteenth century was the introduction of managers, rather than owners or tenants. These are only really apparent from the Census Enumerators' Returns, as they would otherwise appear in the records as innkeepers. This change mirrors the growing empires of the big brewers with their tied houses.

The duties of a landlord were manifold. Brewing one's own beer was commonplace until the nineteenth century. Many inns provided accommodation and food, which required the organisation of beds and meals, with a kitchen to cope with substantial numbers. Organisations frequently met at inns and expected food and rooms, while the transport system was largely based upon co-operation

between landlords, who kept stables for fresh coach-horses as well as accommodating passengers, booking places, and providing post-chaises for hire mostly for local journeys. Large amounts of cash changed hands, which landlords needed to account for, and they could for this reason act as unofficial banks, lending or securing money for their customers. Lastly there was a huge demand in some inns to service the farmers coming in to market, by stabling their horses, parking their carts, and feeding them at the farmers' 'ordinary'.

## Women and Public Houses

Women have long been associated with public houses but until recently (some might say, still) the relationship has been an uneasy one. Public opinion long doubted the respectability of women who frequented pubs, especially on their own. They might even be prostitutes. Conversely, places of transit were good bases for prostitutes, so many of the seedier inns of a town, such as those in China Street, Bridge Lane, and especially St George's Quay, offered a base to both prostitutes and petty criminals, their pimps.

Yet pubs could not run without women. Barmaids were a traditional attraction of these male strongholds; flirtation, emotional support, company and sheer hard drudgery were all expected of them, but this was sharply differentiated from the public attitude to other women, particularly in Victorian times. Many women acted as inn servants or chamber-maids. Women were also cooks, but some occupations, such as that of ostler (looking after the horses), were traditionally male. One of our problems in establishing who did what is that the Census information, which provides a very useful snapshot of inn workers, does not distinguish between different types of domestic service.

Wives traditionally ran the household, dealt with the staff, and kept the hotel functions going (clean beds, prompt food, good service). Research by Julia Stables shows that men who ran pubs in the late nineteenth century were overwhelmingly likely to be married. It was not a role for single men. The role of wives might also extend to daughters, who were sometimes in a position to take over the running of the pub from their fathers. Widows also ran pubs, but in general it seems that women were expected to pass on the pub to be run by a man once things like probate and valuation were sorted out. A good example of this is the **White Lion** in Penny Street, where William Powell took over in about 1822. He must have died young, in 1823, and his widow Jane took on the running of the inn at least until late 1837 and possibly later. In 1844 Thomas Powell, probably her son, was the innkeeper. Clearly Jane was prepared to take on responsibility until he was old enough. There were other women who took on the running of an inn as a long-term occupation, and seem to have been accepted by the other, male, innkeepers. And of course there were some, like Margaret Brown mentioned earlier, who found themselves recurrent licence-holders by default.

Then there were indeed some notable women licensees on their own account. As we have seen, Agnes Starkie ran the **Black Horse** in Common Garden Street from perhaps 1818 until at least 1856. Jane Noon ran the **Royal Oak** in the Market Place, a coaching inn, from 1803 until 1839, herself taking over from Jennet Warbrick, her grandmother, who was there in 1794, and Elizabeth Noon, her mother. Their joint reign lasted at least forty-five years. Jane Noon died in 1851, aged 90. Three women successively ran the **Queen's Head** between 1851 and 1864; Mary Wilson, Mary

Maychell and Hannah Murphy. Were they related? Most likely they were. More often than not, however, women appear as licensees after the death of their husbands, typically for a year or two, but sometimes longer. Many probably escape detection because they changed in the interval between trade directories, one of our best sources, being issued.

The issue of 'respectability' long remained important. In many pubs women could not order drinks at the bar until quite recently, and were expected to be accompanied by a man. The issue has gradually faded as women have become more confident and as society's perceptions have changed, but even today many women are reluctant to go to the bar. Today we see large groups of young women confidently heading off for an evening together, ordering drinks, and doing practically everything that their male counterparts do. But Society has long had, and still surprisingly seems to have, a very ambivalent attitude to women and public houses, even when attitudes have changed enormously in other areas.

# COUNTY & KING'S ARMS

Advertisement for the *County Hotel* and *King's Arms Hotel* in 1889, both at that time run by Samuel Ducksbury. The importance of horses and the large amount of stabling required is apparent from this. It will also be noticed that these large hotels were early adopters of the telephone system, with only the third number in the town!

CHAPTER THREE

# How Do We Know?

## *Reconstructing the Inn*

THE WAY IN WHICH INNS are used and the drinkers are served has changed dramatically over the years, and will continue to change. In many of the newer pubs aimed at the younger market people stand or walk about large open rooms. They drink little beer, favouring alco-pops, or spirits, or proprietary drinks which are drunk out of the bottle. Sometimes jugs are served, perceived to offer better value or to conceal the amount an individual is drinking. Others drink 'shots', highly alcoholic concoctions guaranteed to intoxicate the drinker very swiftly. Sometimes the theme is that of 'sports bar' where matches can be watched on large televisions. The 'sport' is rarely participatory. While the drinking-habits may be new, the trend towards large undivided spaces has been going on for some time, and perhaps originates in large city-centre 'gin-palaces'.

Thirty or forty years ago the pattern was quite different. The tendency in Lancaster was to have a variety of small rooms, often subdivided into alcoves for privacy, with high-backed, leather-covered benches around the walls, and a few loose tables and chairs. The bar was very small, and the service was by waiters, summoned by a bell-push in each room, who fetched orders on trays. It was uncommon for drinkers to stand at the bar, and they were actively discouraged as that got in the way of the waiters. The rooms varied in style and finish, but were all really lounges. It is likely that this pattern goes back to Victorian times.

Before this we have to look at other sorts of evidence. What we see in the late eighteenth and early nineteenth century is rather similar. The bar is often quite insignificant, while there are a great many other rooms where food and drink could be served, many of them doubling as bedrooms when required. Such private rooms became an extension of the bar, and there was a lot less rigidity than today over how they were used. However, the poorest and roughest pubs, such as those in Bridge Lane and China Lane, or in Skerton, probably consisted of little more than the bar with a few seats and tables.

There was also a strong demand for meeting-rooms, usually on upper floors, for groups ranging from the Corporation to Friendly Societies and clubs, such as the Philippi Club, or organisations such as the Masons, who at this stage did not tend to have their own buildings. Publicans were happy to let people meet on their premises because the amount eaten and drunk would serve as room hire. Equally, groups had few other places which were not private or church property in which to meet, and regarded the inn as neutral space. There was also the farmers' 'ordinary' to be held on market and fair days. Crucial to the success of many of these lettings was the availability of stabling, which played a part equivalent to parking today.

China Lane from the Market Street end during demolition work on the west side, c.1895. This short narrow street had six public houses as well as many lodging houses. The *Lord Nelson* on the west side has already gone, to be rebuilt on a different building line. On the east side can be seen the *Spink Bull*, with its projecting lamp. *The Volunteer* and the *Hole in the Wall*, further along, had closed a few years earlier, their licences transferred to more salubrious premises in the suburbs. (Lancaster Library)

The evidence of probate inventories and the borough Rule Books shows that seventeenth- and eighteenth-century inns had many rooms, usually named and rarely numbered, as today. Characteristic were those named after their colour, for example, 'the Green roome' or 'the Blew roome' such as those listed in the inventory of Elizabeth Skirrow of the *Bear & Staff* in 1731 (LRO WRW/A 1731), or of Robert Borranskill of the *Mermaid* in 1726 (LRO WRW/A 1726). The tradition of naming (and placing a device on the door of a room) probably goes back to days of widespread illiteracy. The *Cross Keys* had a 'Cross Keys chamber' in 1720, according to the inventory of Henry Hodgson (LRO WRW/A 1720). The *King's Arms* had a long series of named rooms in 1689 listed in the inventory of Randall Hunter (LRO WRW/A 1689). These were probably based upon their decoration, such as 'the Starr chamber', 'the Half Moone chamber', 'Sun chamber'; or on animals; 'the Fox chamber, 'the Nag's Head'; or mythical creatures, 'the Mare Maid', perhaps appearing as crests on the door. Several of them bore the names of people, either past or present occupants, such as 'Coll. Kirby's chamber' or 'Captain Atkinson's chamber'. By the early nineteenth century these names were being replaced with numbers, as we can see from the entries in the Rule Books for the *Green Dragon* in 1806 and the *White Lion* in 1822.

It is harder to establish the pattern of use in the late seventeenth and early eighteenth century. It seems that it was similar, but the actual innkeeper had a much closer relationship with the principal guests than would a modern hotel manager. Travellers sought local information and news from their innkeeper, who was also regarded as a caterer for all sorts of outside events. Jane Noon of the *Royal Oak* was a landlady who could put on excellent external catering on all occasions. The stock of provisions required by a main inn, and the financial liquidity needed by its proprietor, meant that the innkeeper would act often as an unofficial banker or a provisioner. During and after the siege of Lancaster in 1643 the various forces despoiled the proprietor of the *King's Arms*, James Hardman, of huge quantities of provisions, for which he later sought redress from Parliament. One of his successors, Randall Hunter, who died in 1689, had £7 worth of 'Spanish gold' in his hands, along with £25 in ready cash. Gold coins at that date were of international currency, and were valued by weight, but give an indication of wider trading patterns.

Because of the lack of documentary evidence we can say almost nothing about the earlier state of inns in Lancaster, except by comparison with places where records have survived. There must have been a number of medieval inns, and a few suggestions can be made from the names of those which survived into later times.

What is certain is that over the last four centuries there has been a stratification of inns by social standing or function, from the urbane and well-equipped *King's Arms* or *Commercial Inn*, to the middle-ranking inns of Church Street and Penny Street, serving a largely local function, to the low dives of China Lane, such as the *Hole in the Wall*, regarded by those in authority as little better than thieves' kitchens, and at one time described as 'spit and sawdust' or earlier as 'Tom and Jerry houses'. Even today, when we look around, there are still a very few virtually Victorian pubs, vying for trade with the most stripped-down and open-plan versions of night-clubs, and any attempt to pigeonhole the various types is doomed to failure.

## Sources

There are many sources for a work such as this. The starting point was to search all the trade directories for Lancaster, a mammoth task in itself. This revealed a basic list of inns etc., and of their landlords. It also tied down their locations, within reason. Trade directories are very useful, but not entirely to be relied upon. Information took time to gather, and was often out of date by the time it was printed. Innkeepers changed inns with remarkable rapidity, often between editions of the directory, while names of inns also changed. Other evidence should be preferred if it is available.

This initial work was checked by following up the map evidence, principally that provided by the splendid 1:500 scale Ordnance Survey maps of central Lancaster, produced in 1892, which show every building and property boundary. Most, but not all, of the inns then existing are shown on this. Earlier maps were of some use. Mackreth's of 1778 shows street layouts now gone, as does Binns' of 1821, but inns are not generally distinguished from other buildings. The presence of three inns can be inferred from the map and survey notes published by the late Kenneth Docton, based on the sheets he located in the basement of Towneley Hall. This 1684 survey includes a detailed map and a list of property-owners. The *Sun, Mare Maid* and *Naked Taylor* can be identified from this.

A number of people have been down this particular road before, and have either published articles or have left manuscript notes in the Library. The most outstanding of these are by the late Keith Greenhalgh and the late Eija Kennerley (Lancaster Library, MS 8783). Both of these produced careful and considered notes, but there are also lists by others which are muddled, simply wrong, or contain statements which cannot be checked because they did not reveal their sources. A very useful early source is the reminiscences of Richard Bond, who in an article looked back over seventy years of his life in 1891, reviewing the changes. (R. Bond, 'Memories of seventy years', *Lancaster Philosophical Society Trans.*, 1891) In this he recorded the nett loss of a large number of inns and beerhouses over this period, which he noted contradicted the popular belief in an increase.

The great gap is in documentary evidence before the seventeenth century. Lancaster is generally poor in medieval documents, possibly

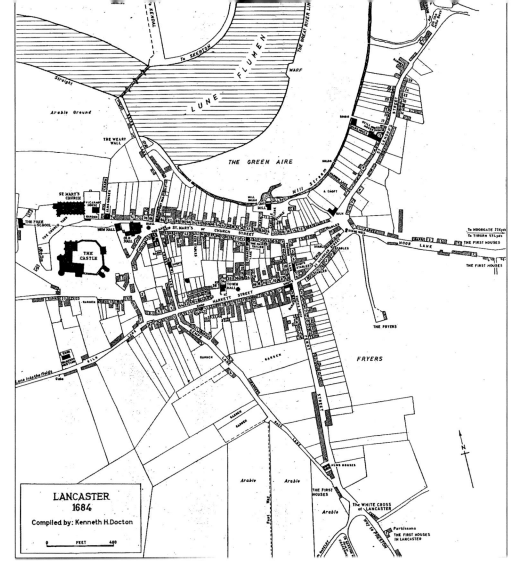

Reconstructed map of Lancaster in 1684, from survey sheets found at Towneley Hall by the late Kenneth Docton. This map shows three inns by name or inference, the *Mare Maid*, *Naked Taylor* and *Sun*, all on Church Street, although this certainly does not indicate the absence of others at the time.

because they were destroyed in one of the many Scottish invasions which the town has suffered, or possibly through the lack of bodies which might have generated them in the first place.

Various records kept by the Borough of Lancaster provide useful information. The Stallenge Rolls record the payment of a fee by non-Freemen in order to trade in Lancaster. For a variety of reasons many innkeepers fell into this category, although some others were undoubtedly Freemen. The records survive between 1685 and 1800, with a substantial gap in the early eighteenth century. Apprentice Rolls, as their name suggests, list the apprenticeships entered into with Lancaster masters. A few sons of innkeepers were apprenticed to other trades, but it was very much a one-way traffic, perhaps showing that innkeeping was not regarded as a very legitimate trade. The Borough Courts were used to settle disputes, generally of a financial nature, between Freemen. The Rule Books which survive between the early eighteenth century and 1822 list goods owned by the defendants in these cases. Many of them were innkeepers, and the detail of some of the lists is phenomenal, allowing us to virtually reconstruct the layout and furnishings of the inn at that date. Where we can check against contemporary newspapers an appearance in the Rule Books seems to have been a sure sign of incipient bankruptcy.

Here are extracts from the Rule Book listing contents of two Lancaster inns:

> Mary Ellershaw [of the *White Lion*, Penny Street], 24th May 1804. It is ordered by this Court that unless the Defendant appear and put in good Bail to this Action within fourteen Days from the date hereof, Sale shall be made of the following Goods and Chattels, to wit, In the Front Parlour, one Oak Dining Table, one Deal Dining Table, one Mahogany Stand, one Deal Buffet, three Bowls with one set of Cups and Saucers, three three [sic] Chairs and one Arm'd one, Dressing Iron, Scales, Smoothing blanket, five Spitting Boxes, two Window Seat Cussions, In The Kitchen Dresser, Clock and Case, a Dozen and a half of Plates, ten Dishes, one Sopha, three Chairs, Seven Brass Candlesticks, four Iron ones, Fire Irons and Fender, one Tin Tea Kettle, toasting Iron, one Mahogany Waiter, one Warming Pan, Smoothing Irons and Heater, one Oven, In the Barr three Plated Pints, one Tankard, Six Ale Glasses, two Pewter Quarts, one Pint, Liquor Measures of all sorts, one Bare Tub, four Waiters, five Case Bottles, one Desk, seven Jugs, one looking Glass, three Punch Ladles, one chest, one Funnel, one Hanging Candlestick, In Back Kitchen one Jack, Nine Dishes, twelve Delf Plates, Brown Mugs and Pots, Eight Pickle Pots, Loaf Tin, two Iron Pans, Knife Box, Copper Boiler, Cloaths Wisket, one pair of Bellows, Baking Utensils, Table Cloth, four Chairs, fender and fire Irons, In the Second Front Parlour one Dale Table, one Mahogany Card Table, nine Chairs, one Mahogany Dining Table, one Looking Glass, Window Cussions, Fire Irons and Fender, three Pictures, the Bells, and two Window Blinds, of the Goods of the said Defendant.

> (Rule Book 1784–1822, 76)

Mary Ellershaw's bankruptcy also appears in the local paper. (*Lancaster Gazette* 26/5/1803)

> John Jackson Victualler [of the *Green Dragon*, Cheapside]
>
> Court 30th January 1806. It is Ordered … Sale shall be made of the following Goods and Chattels, to wit, Garrets, one Sea Chest, three Cheeses, and two small Boxes, First Room, Deal Chest of Drawers and cover, one Swing Glass, Camp Bedsteads and Hangings, one feather Bed, Bolster, and one Pillow, Straw Mattrass, one Pair Sheets, one Pair Blankets, two Bed Quilts, three Chairs, one Liquor Cask, one Liquor case,

one Bed Quilt and set of Bed Hangings, <u>Second Room</u>, Camp bedsteads and Hangings, one feather-Bed, one Bolster and one Pillow, one Pair Sheets, one Pair Blankets, one Stamped Counterpane, one Bed Quilt, three Chairs, one Mahogany Chest of Drawers, Close Stool, one mahogany Wash Stand, one Carpet, Drawers Cover and looking Glass … [four more bedrooms] … <u>Front Parlour</u>, four Pictures, one Pier Glass, nine Chairs, and two Arm'd ones, Floor Cloth, one Mahogany Card and one Snap Tables, one Fender, Poker, one China Bowl, one Jar, a set of Pots etc. and Tea Ware, <u>Back Parlour</u>, Seven Chairs, and one Arm'd Ditto, one Pier Glass, Deal Dining Table, Mahogany Stand, one Drink Table, two Japan Trays, Window Curtains, and Blind, one Fender, one Poker, three Pictures, floor Cloth, and Table Cover, and one Cask a part full of Common Gin, <u>Barr</u>, four Kegs, two plated pints, one Pewter Pint, one Pewter Quart, Six Measures, twenty Glasses, Barr Tub, one Hand Board, one Waiter, Pots, one Cask of Proof Gin, 2 Chairs, one Basket and Sundries, <u>Kitchen</u>, Eight Brass Candlesticks, three Spits, one Brass Mortar, Seven Iron Sticks, one Tea Cannister, Coffee Mill, Candle Box, Tea Kitchen, two Sets of Fire Irons, two Fenders, Warming Pan, Toasting Iron, one Picture, one Jack, one Cask, two Stocking Boards, Pair of Bellows, one Brush, Eight Chairs, one Drink Table, Hop Screw, Mash Nop, Cock, one Gallon Cans, and Sundries, <u>Brew House</u>, one large Copper Boiler, two Copper Pans, one Iron Pan, two Brass Pans, one Copper Can, one Tin Can, one Frying Pan, two Mash Nops, Six Coolers, Toms and Briggs, one Tea Kettle, Toasting Iron, Hop Press, Back Board, and Sundries, <u>Yard</u>, one Bucket, four Casks, four Tubs, one Barrel, three Pigs, a quantity of Coals, and Sundries, <u>First Cellar</u>, Eight, Eighteen Gallon Casks of Ale, one thirty six Gallon of Ale, one thirty six Gallon of Alegar [malt vinegar], five empty Casks, two Casks part full of Ale, two Coolers, and one Can, <u>Second Cellar</u>, three, Eighteen Gallons ^Casks^ [inserted] of Ale, 1, thirty six Gallon Cask of Ale, two Casks of Alegar, two empty Casks, three Working Nops, one Funnel, one Gantree, one Spout, & one Gallon …

(Rule Book 1784–1822, 88)

The Borough also seems to have had its own licensing sessions, but the records of these have not survived.

The Lancashire Record Office holds at least three classes of relevant documents. Probate Inventories and Wills were usually stored together, and the former sometimes record the possessions of innkeepers in similar detail to the Rule Books outlined above, but generally cease to be useful by the 1750s, just at the point when the Rule Books begin.

Here for instance is a list of rooms surveyed by the appraisers for the inventory of Robert Borranskill, gent, in 1726. (LRO WRWA 1726) The accompanying will refers to the 'dwelling house in St Mary Street adjoining the house where he now dwells'. This long list of rooms belongs to the *Mare Maid* or *Mermaid Inn*, which stood at the south-west corner of Church Street and China Lane.

| (rooms listed) | New room |
|---|---|
| Parlour chamber | One sash room |
| Mrs Hornby chamber | 2 bed room |
| Closet | Two sash room |
| Old dining room (containing 17 chairs) | New 2nd green room |
| Gallery chamber | New end closet near the garret |
| White room | Office chamber |
| Blew room | New red room |
| Old garrets | New dining room |
| Green room adjoining old dining room | Shop chamber |
| Garden chamber | Kitchen & scullery (containing 700lbs of |
| Room over brewhouse | pewter vessels) |
| Dark parlour | The backside |
| Bath parlour | Brewhouse |
| Bar parlour | First stable |
| At ye barr | New stable & malt mill |
| Ceiled parlour | (List of silver totalling 184 ounces) |
| Lobby | Ale cellar |
| Street parlour | Other ale cellar |
| Office | Wine cellar |
| New garrets | |

Despite their varied names most of these rooms contained beds. The presence of 'old' and 'new' suggests that this was an old house with a modern extension.

The total value of the goods is £311 5s. 8d.

The probate inventories of Elizabeth Skirrow of the *Bear & Staff* (1731) and of Randall Hunter of the *King's Arms* (1689) are equally instructive.

Parish Registers ought to help with the names of early innkeepers, but unfortunately occupations are rarely given before the mid or late seventeenth century, and of some thirteen innkeepers listed before 1786 only four or five can be assigned to a specific inn. John Bowstead (m. 1759), Anthony Baynes (m. 1775), William Law (1780), Thomas Dixon (1778), Robert Gibson (1781), John Brown (1784), John Hodgson (1784) and William Bird (1784) at present remain unattributed. The same thing goes for wills, where of the thirty-six innkeepers listed between 1748 and 1812, twenty cannot be placed.

There are also the lists of Recognisances issued by the magistrates for the Hundred of Lonsdale. These do not include Lancaster itself, but they do cover Skerton and Scotforth, which until the end of the nineteenth century lay outside the Borough. The merest handful of Recognisances survive for Lancaster in the form of the innkeeper's copy. One such, dated 3 November 1827, relates to John Lythe of the *Golden Ball Inn*. It is signed by Thomas Salisbury and Thomas Giles, both justices, and can be found in Lancaster Library (Library Scrapbook 2, pt 2, 56). Others for John Moss (*Ship*, 1827) and James Hurtley (**Horse & Farrier**, 1828) also survive. Those for Moss and Lythe are handwritten on plain paper, while Hurtley's is a printed form with gaps filled in ink.

Newspapers contain a vast amount of information, from news about inns and innkeepers, and the things that took place on their premises, to advertisements for sales and auctions, sometimes of the inns themselves. The *Lancaster Gazetteer* began in 1801, soon becoming the *Lancaster Gazette*, and was joined by the *Lancaster Guardian* in 1837 (which is still going). Various extracts from local newspapers were issued as books, such as *Lancaster Fifty Years Ago* and *Leaves from Local History*, and the movement of innkeepers recorded in these suggests a much greater turnover than the trade directories indicate. Before 1801 Lancaster news and adverts can appear in the *Cumberland Pacquet*, or the Liverpool or Manchester newspapers. Although the Lancaster newspapers do not appear in the British Library papers now available by random access on-line, various other northern newspapers do, and Lancaster information can be gleaned from them, especially on coaching. Inns themselves often issued handbills recording a change in ownership or tenancy, or some new service. Copies of a number can be found in scrapbooks in Lancaster Library, while a collection in Barrow-in-Furness Record Office, preserved by their printers, the Soulbys, cover large parts of the north west, including Lancaster.

Other libraries contain little gems, such as the list of inns used for 'treating' at the election by Sir Thomas Egerton in 1772, in the John Rylands Library, Manchester. (John Rylands Library, Ryl. Eng. MS 470)

A later source also concerned with elections is the Royal Commission into corrupt practices at the Lancaster election of 1865, where the subject of 'treating' in inns forms the core of the complaint. The *Lancaster Guardian* published a complete transcript of the evidence as a booklet in 1866, while the report of the Royal Commission, published in 1867, runs to 678 pages.

A re-run of sorts occurred in 1896, when complaints were investigated following the election in 1895 of Col. Foster of Hornby Castle, for the Conservatives. A useful list of inns used for 'treating' resulted.

Travellers in the two or three centuries before the coming of the railways often kept journals, many of which have since been published. A selection of extracts appear in this volume. Occasionally other diaries are revealing, such as those of George Hilton, the early eighteenth-century rake and hard drinker. He often noted where he had drunk, such the Lancaster inn not otherwise recorded, which he describes in 1722–23 as 'a pimping ale house calld the *Fox & Dogg* ...' (A. Hillman (transc.), *The Rake's Diary; Journal of George Hilton*, 1994) Two other squires left useful references to Lancaster inns. Thomas Tyldesley, whose diary covers the years 1712–14, lists a number of inns or their landlords (J. Gillow and A. Hewitson (eds),

The *Tyldesley Diary: Personal Records of Thomas Tyldesley during the years 1712–13–14*, 1873), while Nicholas Blundell records his stay at the **Queen's Arms** (now the **King's Arms**) in 1713 while prosecuting a poacher at the Assizes. (M. Blundell, *A Lancashire Squire: The Life of Nicholas Blundell of Crosby 1669–1737*, 2002) The name of this inn must have been altered to honour Queen Anne.

Information preserved in the Census Enumerators' Returns from the regular ten-yearly census, available up to 1901 for study, is another extremely useful resource. The 1881 Census is available as a searchable database on CD, as a result of an enormous transcribing effort by the Mormon Church, while the 1901 Census is accessible via the internet from the National Archives. But all the surviving censuses can now be accessed through the on-line version produced by AncestryLibrary.com, which is conveniently available, free of charge, through the Lancashire Library Service. Other related material is gradually becoming available on the internet, but like the census is rarely presented in a form suited to those who are <u>not</u> studying family history. It can be quite difficult to make general enquiries of these sources as they stand. Only the 1881 Mormon

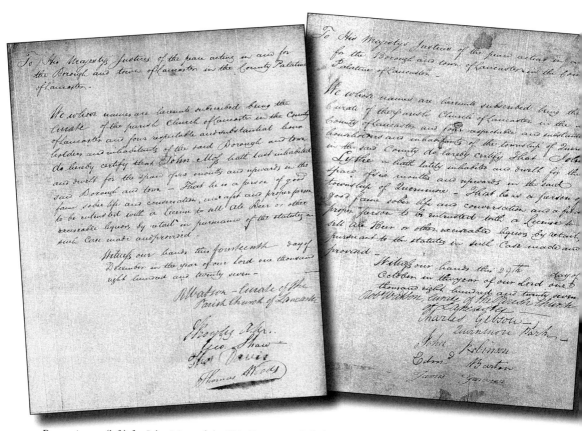

Recognisance (left) for John Moss of the **Ship Inn** to retail ale beer etc., 14 December 1827 and (right) for John Lythe of the **Golden Ball** to sell beer etc., 29 October 1827. (Lancaster Library)

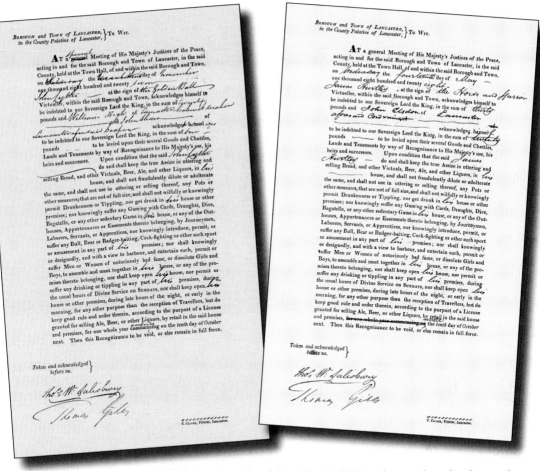

Recognisance (left) for John Lythe of the *Golden Ball*, November 1827, bound with two others in the sum of £20 and (right) for James Hurtley of the *Horse & Farrier* 14 May 1828. (Lancaster Library)

census information is indexed in such a way that occupations rather than surnames can be searched. Local census information from 1841 to 1901 is also available on microfilm in Lancaster Central Library, but there are no short-cuts and the process of searching takes time. This source provides details of age and origin for landlords and their families, and allows us to reconstruct households, including families, lodgers and servants.

Finally, this cannot possibly be the last word on the subject. I have searched many primary sources and most secondary ones, but the local newspapers represent an enormous resource of which I, and others, have barely scratched the surface. These, and other uncatalogued material in various repositories, may well serve to remove some of the perplexities which exist. The growing trend towards searchable catalogues on-line and even scanned original archives may make some of these accessible where they have not previously been. The good news is that on-line access to sources is increasing all the time, but we should still bear in mind the limitations, errors and possible incompleteness of the transcription process.

Inn bill issued by Henry Calvert at the *Old Sir Simon's Inn* in 1829. Curiously there is no charge for beds, although the visitors clearly stayed overnight. At this date the charge seems to have been included in those of meals and horse-keeping. (Lancaster Library)

CHAPTER FOUR

# The Inns

## Beerhouse, Tavern, Inn, Hotel

**W**HAT IS AN INN? The various types of public house have appeared under many names, some accurate and some merely cosmetic. The all-purpose medieval inn provided accommodation, food, drink, stabling and much else besides. Because of their location on main roads or in town centres some no doubt found a ready market with travellers, while others mainly served farmers and other local groups. Inns were controlled from 1552 by licensing, which lay in the hands of the magistrates. Each year innkeepers had to appear before the magistrates and pay in 'recognisances' or a bond for their good behaviour, set in the eighteenth century at £10. They also had to find a friend or colleague who would stand surety for them in a similar amount. This in practice was often another innkeeper, so that individuals paired up to support each other.

From the middle of the eighteenth century the concept of the specialist hotel began to emerge, mainly for travellers on the coach roads, and many purpose-built hotels appeared. The name came to indicate a certain solidity and respectability, so that in the late nineteenth century many large suburban inns were claiming to be hotels, perhaps in order to obtain a license from the magistrates. This is not to say that providing accommodation formed any special part of their activities. So we have town-centre hotels such as the *King's Arms*, clearly offering accommodation as their principal service, and suburban hotels such as the *Bowerham Hotel*, the *Park Hotel* etc., which did not. The nineteenth century also saw a flight of the middle classes from traditional town-centre inns. They had other places to drink, such as clubs, as well as at home, and from the mid-century pubs became distinctively working class.

While the population rose steadily through the Victorian period and many new inns opened, a surprisingly large number also closed. In Lancaster the reminiscences of Richard Bond, written down in 1891, show just how many had gone in his lifetime. He himself made the point that more had gone in his lifetime than had been created, despite the gloomy prognostications of the Temperance lobby. (R. Bond, 'Memories of seventy years', *Lancaster Philosophical Society Trans.*, 1891)

The reasons are many and various. The coming of the railways had destroyed many of the coaching inns from the 1830s onwards, while the removal of soldiers from billets in inns to specialised barracks also had a considerable effect. The secret ballot put a stop to the practice of 'treating' electors with drink, which, as we shall see, had put phenomenal amounts of money in the hands of publicans in the run-up to an election. The gradual discontinuation of payment of wages in pubs, which had led to bouts of drunkeness on paydays, was beneficial to many working class families. Finally, reasonable alternatives to beer, such as cheaper tea and coffee, as well as soft drinks and clean water, made it less attractive. All of this was set against a background of the Temperance Movement, which in the later nineteenth century made huge strides in its influence, and was ignored at their peril by politicians both local and national. Two of the outcomes of this were the opening of Temperance hotels or the conversion of existing ones, and the creation of 'coffee taverns', often subsidised by the issue of tokens, as an alternative to pubs for the working man.

Beerhouses emerged from the Beer Act of 1830, designed to counteract the sale of cheap spirits in working class areas. What were essentially little more than private houses or shops could get a licence for two guineas (£2.10) or three guineas after 1834 (£3.15) to sell beer only, for consumption on the premises. On the whole these were smaller than traditional inns, and in their early days few of them, if any, had a sign or title, mostly being known by the name of their proprietor. But in time the distinction began to be lost. What now seem like traditional inns such as the **Brown Cow** or the **Ring of Bells**, or the **Wagon and Horses** on St George's Quay, all started out as beerhouses, and without a recorded sign. Many of the smaller ones probably came and went, not outliving their original landlord. There was little outlay, and probably not much in the way of goodwill to pass on. In this they were not unlike the small retail shops which changed hands and wares frequently, in contrast to the better-established ones which carried on in a particular trade for generations.

It was the 1869 Wine and Beerhouse Act which brought beerhouses under the control of magistrates, as inns had long been. The cost of licences was now based upon the rateable value, which meant a gradual increase, while an Act of 1872 gave the licensing magistrates power to refuse a licence to any drink retailer who fell foul of the various restrictions, including allowing gambling or prostitution. Consequently the easy life permitted to beerhouses became quite heavily regulated after 1869, and many of the distinctions which divided them from inns were lost. Nonetheless, if we examine beerhouses in the 1901 census, they are always smaller, and employ fewer staff, than inns.

Several inns gather the title 'tavern' at various points in their lives. It is sometimes said that inns were for travellers, while taverns were for locals, but such niceties do not seem to be borne out by the evidence. The *Shakespeare Tavern* had this addition to its title in some directories, but the only tavern to exist at present is probably the *Rose Tavern*, on Freehold. This title does not seem to have any legal distinction, or long-term consistency. In some cases it may well have been the intention to give an antique flavour about the establishment, redolent of Toby jugs and coach lamps, just as the addition of 'Ye Olde' to the name was supposed to do.

It is interesting today to see the clash between differing sorts of marketing, with an old-fashioned and traditional appeal to the older drinkers, that of the quintessential English 'pub' which never existed, contrasting with the cool and sophisticated naming and decorating of bars intended for young drinkers, who have a very different approach to a night out. The old differences between inns, where they survive, are being rendered irrelevant by the opening of new bars or conversion of existing ones, which are part night-club, part restaurant and part wine or coffee-bar, aided by the culture of all-day licensing.

Changes to licensing in 2003 mean that the name of the licensee now is often the name of the company which owns the pub, rather than that of an individual, although many individual licensees are also recorded, where there are 'free' houses. This means that in future it will be much harder to track innkeepers and managers as they move around. Most of those holding licences before 2003 were able to transfer directly to the new system under so-called 'grandfather's rights'.

## Inn Names

Originally inns were given distinctive names which could be reinforced for the largely illiterate clientele with a memorable symbol, or an inn sign, painted by one of a number of itinerant painters.

The names could also be used to reinforce the connection between an inn and the occupational group which frequented it. Many trades and industries were very localised to particular streets. Examples of trade connections are the long list of *'Arms'*, such as the *Farmers', Stonemasons', Cabinetmakers', Coachmakers'* (both of the last two being situated in St Leonardgate, where Gillow's and Dunn's carried out their respective businesses). There were also the *Sawyers', Carpenters', Butchers', Hatters', Moulders'* (in Wood Street, near two foundries), *Painters', Mechanics', Spinners'* (in Aldcliffe Lane near Queen's Mill) and *Cordwainers'* (boot and shoemakers) *Arms*. Then there were more indirect connections such as the *Boot & Shoe* (Market Street, Scotforth and Skerton) and the *Golden Fleece* and *Rainbow*, associated with cobblers, woolcombers and dyers respectively. The *Swan with two Necks* (usually interpreted as the Swan with two Nicks, its mark of ownership), is another ancient name recalling the custom of swan-upping, or gathering and marking swans. This sign is that of the Vintners' Company, while the *Three Tuns* is that of the Dyers'. The *Wheatsheaf* is likewise the sign of the Bakers' Gild.

Since Lancaster had no trade gilds as such, apart from a very brief period in the late seventeenth century, these would have used the arms of the London companies.

Inn names tend to fall into natural groups. There are the royal names – *Albert Inn, Victoria Inn, Prince William Henry, William IV, King Edward, Alexandra, George*, and more indirect royal symbols such as *The Feathers* (for the Prince of Wales) and *White Hart* (for Richard II).

Arms or livery badges of notable families include the *Eagle & Child* (Stanley), *Talbot* (Earl of Shrewsbury), *Bear & Staff* (Earl of Warwick), *Swan* (Bohun), *White Lion* (Duke of Norfolk), *Red Lion* (John O'Gaunt) and *Green Dragon* (Herbert), as well

as obvious local gentry names such as *Marton, Dalton* and *Hamilton*. There was also the *Three Legs of Mann*, arms of the Isle of Man, but also from the seventeenth century associated with the Stanleys, Earls of Derby, who were Lords of Man. Three or four of these armorial symbols go back to prominent families in the Wars of the Roses in the late fifteenth century, and it is possible that they indicate the sites of ancient inns. The *Crooked Billet* is an ancient sign, but whether it is the badge of a noble family is not known.

Many names show a taste for animal portraits, such as the *Brown Cow, Spink Bull, Gray Horse, Fox & Goose,* or *Bay Horse,* which went down well with a farming community. 'Spink' seems to be a dialect word for 'spotted'. Occasionally inns commemorated spectacular prize beasts in the early days of selective breeding and fattening such as the *Craven Heifer* (bred at Bolton Abbey and famous in 1807–12) or the *Durham Ox* (bred at Ketton near Darlington in 1795 and exhibited around the country in 1801–10). Both were the subjects of popular prints which made attractive inn signs, and their dates of origin can be quite firmly fixed.

Opposite the Theatre, built in 1782, stood the appropriately named *Shakespeare Tavern*, now, alas, no longer an inn. Other historical characters commemorated include two figures from opposite sides in the 1745 Jacobite Rebellion: *Old Sir Simon* (Lord Lovat), Jacobite, and the *Duke of Cumberland*, brother of the King, leader of the government forces and eventual victor. *Lord Nelson* and *Wellington* were both heroes of the Napoleonic Wars. The *Royal Oak* commemorates Charles II's narrow escape by hiding in an oak tree at Boscobel after the battle of Worcester in 1651. Oak-apple Day used to celebrate this occasion every 29 May with feasting and the ringing of bells.

A small group of inn signs prosaically record their proximity to some now-vanished feature, such as the *Cockpit*, *Cattle Market* and *Tramway*, the latter recording the Lancaster and District horse trams, which started nearby.

A small but colourful group include those signs which illustrate proverbs or stories, such as *The Naked Tailor*, *Bird in Hand* or the *Mermaid*. The naked tailor is probably a reference to the way that business takes all the time, leaving no room for personal work, as in 'the cobbler's child goes barefoot'. The bird in hand is clearly related to the proverb 'a bird in the hand is worth two in the bush'. Mermaids were popular inn signs, showing a semi-naked woman with a fish tail, holding a comb and a looking-glass in her hand, an ancient symbol of vanity and the snares of the flesh. *The Gate Hangs Free* (or *Well*) seems to have been quite a widespread inn name, and its sign usually carried a verse to signify the meaning.

Possibly the oldest group, although as no early records survive for Lancaster we cannot prove it, are those signs which incorporate religious motifs, such as the *Mitre* (symbol of a bishop), *Cross Keys* (the symbol of St Peter, and by extension of the diocese of York), *Red Cross* and *White Cross*, both which may mark ownership by monastic or military orders such as the Templars.

All these names allowed colourful signs to be displayed. Shops and even private houses used signs to indicate where they were, when street numbers were not in use. In London the quantity of hanging signs, which sometimes fell on passers-by, caused such a problem that there was an ordinance against them in 1763, resulting in the fixing back of signs to buildings rather than allowing them to hang over streets. There is some evidence that in other towns the same battle was taken up, including Lancaster, where the Corporation made a similar rule in 1764.

Two inn signs are specifically mentioned among personal possessions of the landlords in the Rule Book of the Borough Court, that of the *Golden Talbot* (a talbot was a sort of dog), China Lane, in 1766, and that of the *Ram's Head*, Cheapside, in 1764. (Rule Book 1736–84, 29–31, 38)

Some inn signs were political in intent. 'Blue' as a prefix was often used to indicate support of the Whig or Liberal party. Not all 'Blue' names are however political. Primrose was then used as a colour for political favours by the Tory or Conservative party, as in the 'Primrose League', though this rarely appears in pub names.

In more recent times inn names have been subject to rapid change, either to meet a new fashion or to appeal to a new group of users, generally younger. In the 1990s there was a fashion for Irish-named fun-pubs, and Lancaster duly obliged with *Fibber McGee's* (formerly the *Slip Inn*) and with *Paddy Mulligan's* (formerly the *White Horse*). The latter has already changed back to an earlier manifestation, *Stonewell Tavern*. Since then there has been a further move to reposition inns within the market, by for instance suggesting that they are peaceful or more sophisticated than the rowdy youth-pubs. Names such as *The Lounge, Vines* or *Moods* are probably the result of this move. Even during the period of research for this book some old inns have changed their names twice. It is hard to predict whether these are short-term or whether they represent an irreversible change in style and clientele. Along with name-changes there has been a great deal of redesign, to try to give the impression of a wine-bar, a night-club, a licensed restaurant or some other archetype. Indeed, the old divisions between inn, hotel, beer house etc. have not reflected reality for a long time.

In producing the Gazetteer I had great difficulty with consistency in names. Old names were used years after a name-change, while many had nicknames, such as *The Tubs* or *The Vaults* which were used by their regulars instead of the official one. The *Golden Lion* is also sometimes known as the *Whittle Springs* after its nineteenth-century brewery! There is no satisfactory way of including all these elements, except by cross-referencing.

## Numbers of Inns and Public Houses in Lancaster

The sources for this information are principally trade directories. In some instances they separate hotels or principal inns from the rest, while in others they list beerhouses on their own.

| | | | |
|---|---|---|---|
| 1794 | 51 | 1851 | 66 + 30 beer houses |
| 1805 | none listed | 1856 | 66 |
| 1809 | only 3 listed | 1864 | 56 |
| 1814 | only 4 listed | 1871–72 | 60 |
| 1816–17 | 3 listed | 1881 | 56 + 19 beer houses |
| 1818 | 5 + 60 | 1886 | 55 + 20 beer houses |
| 1822 | 6 + 57 | 1889–90 | 48 + 17 beer retailers |
| 1828–29 | 61 + 4 inc. Scotforth | 1896 | 47 + 19 beer retailers |
| 1834 | 5 + 59 + 19 beer houses | 1901 | 58 + 17 beer retailers |

Richard Bond, in his recollections of the previous 70 years, written in 1891, lists 46 inns and beerhouses which had ceased to exist during his lifetime, while only six new ones had appeared in that time, despite the great rise in population. There are some discrepancies, in that Bond suggests that in about 1836 the total of licensed houses was 117 for a population of 12,163. The numbers from the directories give nothing like this figure, and never higher than one hundred of all types. The beerhouses represent the largest variable and no doubt many came and went in a short period.

## Lancaster's Oldest Inns

My criteria for making this judgement are that the inn has to still exist and has to have had a continuous existence up to the present day, even if this involves changes of name. Some of these inns have been rebuilt, but all on the same site. There are seven in total. Two begin in the seventeenth century, the remainder in the eighteenth century.

| | | |
|---|---|---|
| *King's Arms* | Market Street | 1640 – date |
| *Sun Inn* | Church Street | 1680s – date |
| *1725 Tapas Bar (Blue Anchor)* | Market Square | 1725 – date |
| *Duke of Lancaster (Black Bull)* | Church Street | 1743 – date |
| *Last Orders (Nag's Head)* | Church Street | 1756 – date |
| *Fibber McGee's (Slip Inn)* | James Street | 1776 – date |
| *Three Mariners (Carpenters' Arms)* | Bridge Lane | 1778 – date |

Of these, until its recent name-change to *1725*, the **Blue Anchor** seemed to be the only one to retain both its original name and building, albeit being much extended, and so it could still be legitimately claimed as the oldest inn in continuous use in Lancaster.

Of those inns which have now disappeared one could hazard a guess that one of the oldest could well be the *Cross Keys* in Market Street, recorded from 1632. Its sign, that of the keys of St Peter, and hence of the archdiocese of York, may very well hark back to the Middle Ages. Documentary evidence for its early existence is so far lacking, and although we have evidence for earlier innkeepers, there is nothing in property deeds and no other documents to tie down which inns they occupied.

## Skerton and Scotforth

Until the end of the nineteenth century the two villages of Skerton and Scotforth lay outside the boundaries of Lancaster. They were incorporated in Improvements Acts of 1888 and 1900. The numbers that they added to the borough's population were not huge, but the character of the borough was affected. Previously Lancaster had been defined by quite tight boundaries, a core of streets surrounded on three sides by the town fields. The remaining side, the north, was defined by the river Lune. During the nineteenth century Lancaster had started to spread out over its fields, first by ribbon development along the roads that led west and south, then by denser developments over fields to the east. The tentacles gradually led out to Scotforth, which still remained a relatively rural community, with a very large agricultural element to the township to its south and east. Skerton was rather different. It occupied a relationship similar to that enjoyed by Kirkland to Kendal, i.e. outside the control of the borough, but on its very doorstep. A lower standard of building control took place in Skerton and there was much less restriction of trade, which probably accounts for the traditionally high number of travellers and horse dealers among its population.

Skerton had many inns and beerhouses, and they and those of Scotforth fell outside the legislation of the borough, so their innkeepers had to obtain recognisances from the magistrates of the Hundred of Lonsdale, along with other rural villages. Consequently they have a source of information which does not survive for the older core of Lancaster. Opposite are four examples. The first two have no inn names. In each case the innkeeper and a friend (in many cases an innkeeper in Lancaster proper) had to pay over a £10 surety for the good conduct of their inn.

Many of Skerton's inns lay along Main Street, which lay parallel to the river but set back from it. Their names often match those of inns in the town centre, such as the *Blue Anchor, Boot & Shoe, Black Bull* or *Black Horse*. There was little likelihood of confusion. Only a few of Skerton's inns survive today. By contrast Scotforth only seems ever to have had two inns, the *Boot & Shoe* and *Bowling Green*, which both survive, and were clearly intended to serve passing trade along the main road, now the A6. A third inn, sometimes recorded in trade directories as within Scotforth, was the *Hamilton Arms*, but it was actually in Conder Green and is now the *Stork*.

| 1796 | 1823 |
|---|---|
| **Skerton** | **Skerton** |
| W Dixon | Wm Carter, *Millstone* |
| J Toulmin | Jane Clough, *Red Cross* |
| Ann Gell? | John Longfield, *Bird in Hand* |
| Nicholas Parkinson | Richard Myerscough, *Black Bull* |
| Chr Mounsey | Richard Warbrick jun, *Blue Anchor* |
| Margaret Woodhouse | Richard Wadeson, *Carpenters' Arms* |
| John Longfield | |
| | **Scotforth** |
| **Scotforth** | Richard Dickson, *Boot & Shoe* |
| John Griffin | John Griffin, *Bowling Green* |
| (LRO QSB3/132) | (LRO QSB3/160/5/1) |

| 1815 | 1828 |
|---|---|
| **Skerton** | **Skerton** |
| Rachel Mawson | Wm Carter, *Millstone* |
| John Longfield | John Longfield, *Bird in Hand* |
| Jonathan Tiffin | Richard Myerscough, *Black Bull* |
| Wm Carter | Richard Warbrick, *Blue Anchor* |
| Richard Nuttall | Thos Wilson, *Red Cross* |
| Thos Clough | Richard Waidson, *Carpenters' Arms* |
| | |
| **Scotforth** | **Scotforth** |
| Richard Dixon | Richard Dixon, *Boot & Shoe* |
| Timothy Longton | John Griffin, *Bowling Green* |
| (LRO QSB3/151 Lonsdale) | (LRO QSB 3/168/4/1) |

## Architecture

Most of the older inns in Lancaster cannot easily be distinguished from houses, and that is probably how they originated. Mostly the size was limited by the width and depth of the medieval burgage-plots. It is unlikely that any but the largest were purpose-built. Even some of the larger inns with twenty or thirty rooms may well have been converted out of two or three adjacent houses. Until the late seventeenth century most buildings in Lancaster were timber-framed, but in quite a short time nearly all were rebuilt in stone. One or two inns such as the *Sun*, in Church Street, or the *Red Lion*, in Lower Church Street, seem to have remained in older timber buildings for most of the eighteenth century, but both were eventually rebuilt in stone.

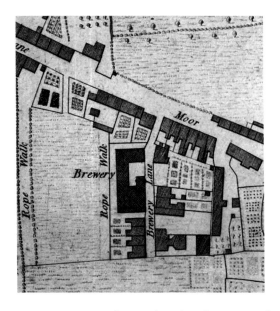

The Brewery in Moor Lane, from Mackreth's map of Lancaster in 1778. The Brewery had a very good spring of water, and so remained in use for several centuries, indeed until 1999, when finally closed by Mitchells.

Stables and large yards may have been the main difference between an inn and a private house, but in a town such as Lancaster with its long medieval burgage-plots space was not always a problem. Coaching inns in particular had to be well equipped, but many inns had to accommodate farmers' horses and carts on market days and required extensive stabling. The *Commercial Inn* in the Market Place was one such, built on the site of several earlier houses, including 'Mr Hornby's Great House'. (LCC Deeds 85/3) Even after it ceased to be an inn the yard proved useful to the Corporation Fire Brigade for storage of hoses and ladders, as well as providing space for the horses and the fire engines.

In the nineteenth century a particular type of pub began to be built. Purpose-built and large, with ornate decoration, often including stained glass (another important local industry), they set out to impress, rather as cinemas did later. They were meant to be larger than life, to give a glimpse of another, grander, world. In London they were known as 'gin-palaces', but in Lancaster the connection with gin was slight. Large pubs such as these began to appear in the suburbs, such as the *Moorlands Hotel* on the new Moorlands Estate or the *Bowerham Hotel* at Bowerham, and were all eminently respectable. Indeed the designation 'hotel' was an aid to respectability. The design was followed by other pubs in the town centre,

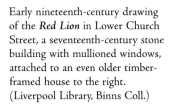

Early nineteenth-century drawing of the *Red Lion* in Lower Church Street, a seventeenth-century stone building with mullioned windows, attached to an even older timber-framed house to the right. (Liverpool Library, Binns Coll.)

such as the Edwardian rebuild of the *Black Bull* in Church Street (now the *Duke of Lancaster*).

Eminent local architects such as Paley & Austin were pleased to work with the local brewers, such as Mitchells and Yates & Jackson. Edwardian remodelling of the southern approaches of the town led to the rebuilding of the two large inns there, the *White Cross* and the *Alexandra*, as a deliberate piece of urban planning, still very impressive today.

Other brewers often used their own favourite architects and so exported their style to towns such as Lancaster, regardless of the local vernacular.

In the late twentieth and early twenty-first century there has been a net loss of pubs in the city centre, while many of the newer bars and night-clubs are conversions of other existing buildings. There is, as a consequence, no single distinctive style.

## Temperance and Teetotalism

Temperance was a powerful movement in the nineteenth century, intent on reducing the drinking of alcohol. It was particularly strong in Lancashire, with a focus on Preston with the rise of Teetotalism, which preached total abstention rather than moderation. While moderation had been preached in earlier times the complete abstention from alcohol was only made possible by pure water supplies and the fall in the price of tea and coffee, which put them within the reach of all. Small (weak) beer had earlier been the universal drink, and was usually safer than water.

It was widely recognised that drink was the enemy of working people, even if it was one of few ways to escape from the squalor of day-to-day life. A man who drank was denying his family food and shelter – they could rarely afford both. Well-to-do drinkers were less stigmatised. They could perhaps afford to drink without damaging their family, but even here the risks of self-indulgence and the slippery slope leading to alcoholism were frequently shown in moralistic paintings.

Even as early as the 1790s the dangers of drink were becoming a public concern. A leaflet issued with the support of Lancaster magistrates in the 1790s was entitled 'The Contrast' (Library, Scrapbook 2, pt 4, 29) and showed the contrast between good and bad landlords. The former ceased to serve their customers if they seemed drunk, and did not allow gaming or open on Sundays at times of divine service. In particular they would only serve a maximum of two pints to working men, to avoid the consequences to their families. The latter were the reverse of all these, and carried on serving drink to men who could not afford it and who would not be fit to work in the morning. The arguments have a curiously timeless ring to them. It is not clear what prompted the campaign.

Temperance was about moderation, but the 'Teetotallers' were absolute. Moderates, so-called 'little drop drinkers', were often ridiculed.

Various actions were taken to gain recruits and to take everyday life out of the public house. Children were encouraged to take the pledge (never to drink alcohol) and to join the Band of Hope, established in 1847. Working men, especially piece-workers and fishermen, who were traditionally paid out in pubs, were encouraged to draw their pay elsewhere. One way of achieving this was to establish coffee houses where working men could meet without drinking alcohol, while Temperance Hotels and lodging houses, of which Lancaster had several, were intended to provide a drink-free environment for the many single men who occupied them. Tokens were issued to working men allowing them to buy non-alcoholic drinks

## BOROUGH of LANCASTER.

☞ Many of the Magiſtrates of this Kingdom at their late Licenſings have thought proper to deliver to every Publican a Copy of the following Paper; and have directed that it be placed in ſome conſpicuous part of every Public Houſe, as a ſtanding juſtification of their conduct in determining to keep Good Order, and as a ſtanding reproof to them in caſe of their miſbehaviour.

### THE CONTRAST.

THE true Uſe of Inns, Ale-Houſes, and Victualling-Houſes is to afford Refreſhment and Lodging to Travellers; to accommodate Perſons meeting on neceſſary buſineſs; to entertain Soldiers on his Majeſty's Service; and to ſupply the wants of ſuch as are not Houſeholders themſelves, or are unable to procure victuals or drink in larger quantities: But not to harbour idle, lewd, and diſorderly perſons.

Many Good Laws have been framed to prevent theſe abuſes; that the Poor may not be reduced to beggary by the temptations held forth to them by evil-minded Publicans; who to promote their own advantage, are totally regardleſs of the Laws.

The difference between a good and a bad Publican will beſt be diſtinguiſhed by the following                    CONTRAST:

*A GOOD Publican*

Suffers no perſon to tipple in his houſe on the LORD's Day; nor any one to come and reſort main there except Travellers, and ſuch as reſort thither on urgent buſineſs.

*A good Publican* ſuffers no perſon reſorting to his houſe, except Travellers, to remain after Nine o'Clock in Winter, nor after Ten in Summer.

*A good Publican* ſuffers no liquor to be drawn for any perſon who appears to have had more than enough already.

*A good Publican* ſuffers no perſon frequenting his houſe, to remain tippling more than one hour in any part of the day, except Travellers.

*A good Publican* ſuffers no quantity of beer exceeding two pints to be drawn for any one perſon of the deſcription of labourers or mechanics, at any one time; ſuch refreſhment being fully ſufficient, and the expence of it as much as can properly be afforded.

*A good Publican* ſuffers no perſon to remain in his houſe who uſes profane or ſeditious language, breeds diſturbance, and wiſhes to promote quarrelling, fighting, or diſorderly behaviour.

*A good Publican* ſuffers no kind of Gaming whatſoever to be practiſed in his houſe; nor any implements for Gaming to be on any part of his premiſes.

*A good Publican* is a very reputable Member of the Community; a willing Promoter of Public Service, often at his own great loſs; and affords an uſeful accommodation to the ſober and induſtrious, who in a well-ordered place of reſort, enjoy the comforts of Society, and that relaxation from buſineſs and care, to which honeſt [...]

*A BAD Publican*

Encourages his thoughtleſs Neighbour to frequent his houſe inſtead of the Church, and to miſpend the time which ought to be given to the ſervice of God, and the money which ought to be applied to the ſupport of his Wife and Family.

*A bad Publican* keeps his houſe open to a very late hour; encouraging his Cuſtomers to ſtay and drink to exceſs, thereby diſqualifying themſelves for the buſineſs of the following day.

*A bad Publican* gives drink to the drunken, and thereby increaſes both their guilt and their ſhame.

*A bad Publican* ſuffers the idle and drunken to continue tippling hour after hour, and ſometimes even from morning till night, and from night till morning, attentive only to his own intereſt; and in utter defiance of the Laws, which have ordained a penalty of 3s. 4d. to the perſon tippling, and 10s. to the Publican that ſuffers it.

*A bad Publican* draws pint after pint, and quart after quart, though he knows he is depriving the poor imprudent Tippler's Wife and Children of what would otherwiſe be employed in procuring them decent raiment and neceſſary food.

*A bad Publican* has no objection to profane talk or ſeditious Meetings; nor to fighting, whether upon a ſtage or off it; nor to any barbarous paſtime, which may call a multitude of perſons together—to empty his caſk and to fill his purſe.

*A bad Publican* has many devices for Amuſement, as he calls it; ſuch as Dice, Cards, Shuffle-Board, Skittles, Billiard-Tables, &c. to the encouragement of Gambling, and the ruin of his Cuſtomers.

*A bad Publican* is a very great nuiſance to ſociety, and deſerves to be ſuppreſt, as an enemy to Virtue, Sobriety, and good order; as one that is particularly adverſe to the beſt intereſts of a very valuable part of the Community, both in this world and the next.

The Contrast (between good and bad landlords), issued by the Corporation of Lancaster in 1796. Its provisions reflect those in the later printed forms for landlords' recognisances, and indeed some of them are still relevant today. (Lancaster Library)

No pink elephants here! Sanger's Circus comes to town in the 1890s and passes *Scott's Temperance Hotel*, opposite the *King's Arms*, in Market Street. This building was later demolished and the rear of the site is now occupied by the *Merchants*. Immediately to its right was the Lancaster Coffee Tavern, another Temperance initiative. (Courtesy of Lancaster City Museum part of Lancashire Museums)

in the coffee houses, as an incentive to move away from alcohol. Many of these tokens still exist, and are collectable.

Powerful Temperance landowners and magistrates often worked to take away inn licences, resulting in many villages which had only a Temperance hotel (such as Quernmore or Melling) or reduced licensing hours. Gressingham lost its only pub in the 1870s, largely through a Temperance lobby led by the Vicar.

Just as it seemed most powerful the Temperance movement began to lose strength. Some saw it as a paternalistic means of controlling the working man. Equally it was unpopular with much of the middle class because of the assault on freedom of choice. Like the Prohibition Movement in America, it aroused strong opposition. It has however left a considerable heritage behind, and part of the reaction to binge drinking today can be traced back to these antecedents.

With modern prosperity it is difficult for us to appreciate fully the scorn in which a Victorian drinker, a 'boozer', was held by the respectable working class, as his indulgence was at the expense of his family, and for the artisan, perhaps his business as well.

The *(Royal) King's Arms Hotel*, for over three centuries Lancaster's premier inn, on the corner of Market Street and King Street. This tall and rather fussy but undeniably impressive building replaced its Georgian predecessor in 1879–82. Its footprint owes much to the shape of the rather random collection of houses that had been taken into the earlier inn. It once had a very extensive range of stables and coach-houses extending along King Street.

CHAPTER FIVE

# Gazetteer of Inns and Public Houses in Lancaster

THIS IS INTENDED TO be a comprehensive list of all the beerhouses, inns, taverns, pubs or hotels which have existed in Lancaster over the last four centuries, the extent of records. Inevitably a few will have been missed, misidentified, muddled or even invented. I can only apologise for errors, and hope that this will form the basis for further work.

Many inn names have changed over the years. Those which have been wholly renamed are cross-referenced in this list. Those which appear under variants are more difficult to track, as *Fleece* may have been the more common name for *Golden Fleece* and *Bull* may appear frequently for *Black Bull* or *Spink Bull*, while many inns have at one time had 'Old' put in front of the name, as in *Old Cross Keys*, or even worse, *Ye Olde Cross Keys*. On the other hand *Old Sir Simon* was a real person, not an old inn with the sign of Sir Simon. The *Slip Inn* and *Ship Inn* are often confused in directories, as are *Sun* and *Swan*. If you cannot find a name, look at possible variants. It is impossible to be completely consistent when the sources themselves are not. Some at least reflect the tendency of drinkers to shorten or simplify the name of their favourite pub.

In this list street numbers are based on those in the 1896 street directory, which is the nearest in date after the 1892 1:500 Ordnance Survey, enabling the two to be used together. Inevitably a few inns closed before that date, or were rebuilt on new sites after it, in which case no number may be given. In a few cases I have used either the 1889–90 or the 1901 street directory as a substitute, either when the 1896 directory was defective, or when some area such as China Lane was demolished and rebuilt around that time.

The pace of change in recent years has made it very difficult to keep up with alterations of name, owner and even function. Even as I am writing these words old inns are closing, losing their identity, or changing to night clubs or tapas bars. The details are as correct as it has been possible to be at time of writing. Most space has been allocated to the more historic establishments, but recent additions are noted for the sake of completeness.

---

*Albert Inn* (now *Vine & Hops*) (Beerhouse)                                                84 King Street

This beerhouse, standing on the west side of Upper King Street first appears in 1881.

In 1936 the front part was rebuilt. (LRO deposited plans no 5846) In 1986 it was closed by the official receiver due to bankruptcy, but subsequently reopened and in 2003 was renamed *The Vines*, later *Vine & Hops*.

| | |
|---|---|
| 1881 | (Census) Christopher Foster |
| 1886–96 | Richard Clapham |
| 1901–13 | Mrs Anne E. Clapham |
| 1934 | Elizabeth Smith |
| 1956–57 | ? |
| 1970 | C. Gough |
| –1986 | Irene Gough |
| 1986 | Closed by official receiver |
| ? | Re-opened |
| 2003 | Renamed *The Vines* wine bar |
| 2006 | N. M. Arebi |

*Vine & Hops*, King Street.

### Alexandra Hotel (originally *Corporation Hotel*, now *Rɘvolution*)    Penny Street

In 1901–2 Lancaster Corporation remodelled the southern approach to the town, which involved demolition of quite a lot of property in the upper part of Penny Street, including the old *Corporation Arms* and *White Cross* (qv). Two new and substantial hotels were built on new sites facing Penny Street bridge over the canal, the *Corporation Hotel* and *White Cross*. Both were subsequently renamed, the former after a very short time to *Alexandra*, probably to commemorate the accession to the throne of Edward VII and Alexandra in 1902. The *White Cross* later became the *Farmers' Arms*, and later the *Penny Street Bridge* (qv). In 2003 the *Alexandra* was renamed *Rɘvolution*, with a reversed 'e' to emulate the Russian letter and give a revolutionary flavour.

| | |
|---|---|
| 1901–2 | Opened |
| c1920s | Parsons |
| 1929 | A. S. Ducksbury |
| 1934 | R. L. Parsons |
| 1956–57 | ? |
| 2003 | Now named *Rɘvolution* |
| 2006 | Inventive Leisure Services Ltd. |

*Alexandra Hotel/Rɘvolution*, Penny Street.

### Anchor Inn (see *Blue Anchor*)    Market Street

### Athenaeum Hotel (formerly *Black Cat*)    95–7 St Leonardgate

| | |
|---|---|
| 1901 | (Census) Robert J. Gardner |
| 1913 | H. Hunter |
| 1929 | ? |
| 1934 | George Haworth |
| 1956–57 | ? |
| 1961 | Demolished |

## Barley Mow ?

1772      William Bentham (Egerton MS, John Rylands Library)
1782      Robert Wright (Stallenge Rolls)
1783–87    Michael Cooper (Stallenge Rolls)

## Bay Horse (then *Castle Hotel*, then *Kampus*, now *The Pub*)      45 China Street

One of many inns to be found at one time in China Lane, in the nineteenth century a very rough and insalubrious area, it stands on the east side, near the southern end. First recorded in 1794 it lasted for more than a century before being bought by Yates' Brewery in 1897 (Library MS 1043) and being rebuilt in the same year as part of the road widening, replanning and renaming to China Street. (LRO deposited plans no 1592). The rebuilt inn was named *Castle Hotel*, and is the sole survivor of the many inns of old China Lane. In 2004 it was renamed *Kampus*, then in 2006 *The Pub*, surely one of the least imaginative names possible.

1794      Elizabeth Bateman
1818–22    Matthew Gardner
1825–28    John Dodd
1834      Thomas Thexton
1844–51    John Morland
1854      John McCann
1864      Thomas Smith
1871–72    Betsy Smith
1881      George Holden
1886–90    John Hartley
1897      Conveyance J. S. Ducksbury to
         Yates Brewery, (Library MS
         1043)

(see *Castle Hotel*)

*Bay Horse/Castle/The Pub*, China Street.

## Bear & Staff (Hotel)　　　　　　　　　　　　　　　　　　　　5 Penny Street

Two old inns stood side by side on the east side of Penny Street, just south of Horseshoe Corner. These were the *Bear & Staff* and the *Queens Hotel* (formerly *White Lion*) (qv). Both have now gone. The *Bear & Staff* is first recorded in 1731.

For many years from 1791 to 1818 it was kept by Sergeant Rippon, an officer of the Corporation, and much Corporation business was done here, as well as it being the venue for the Mayor's Venison Feast up to 1803. In 1825 the following carriers ran from here: Robert Redmayne for Kirkby Lonsdale every Wednesday and Saturday, Thomas Butler for Ulverston every Tuesday and Friday as the tides permitted, and Thomas Saul for Wray every Monday, Thursday and Saturday. In 1837 the landlord, C. Kelsall, announced the start of coaches over the sands from his inn to Ulverston (*Lancaster Guardian*, 9/9/1837). A sale catalogue survives for the inn in 1899 (Library S1/39). In 1936–37 it was demolished to make way for Woolworths' new store.

| | |
|---|---|
| 1731 | Probate Inventory of Elizabeth Skirrow, innkeeper (LRO WRW/A 1731) |
| 1748 | Robert Parkinson |
| 1761–77 | William Howson (Egerton MS, John Rylands Library; will in LRO, WRW/A 1777) |
| 1778–84 | Cuthbert Baines (Stallenge Rolls) |
| 1791–1818 | William 'Sergeant' Rippon (Stallenge Rolls; Library Scrapbook 6, pt 1, 32v) |
| 1820–22 | Thomas 'Sergeant' Camm (declared bankrupt. Inn to let, *Lancaster Gazette*, 11/5/1822) |
| 1825–32 | Christopher Dodd (Library, Scrapbook 3, 135; will in LRO WRW/A 1832) |
| 1834 | Charles Kelsall |
| 1839–44 | Mrs Mary Cowbourn (*Lancaster Gazette*, 29/6/1839) |
| 1851 | Thomas Dixon |
| 1854 | Ann Davidson |
| 1864–65 | John Bibby (1865 Election petition) |
| 1871–72 | M. Richmond |
| 1881–82 | (Census) (Library, billhead) Edward Huntington |
| 1886–90 | Mrs Sarah Thexton |
| 1896–1901 | A. G. Harrison |
| 1913 | W. Huntington |
| 1929 | ? |
| 1934 | Edward Caton |

## Bee Hive　　　　　　　　　　　　　　　　　　　　　　　　　　Church Street

| | |
|---|---|
| 1844–47 | Robert Speight (will LRO WRW/A 1847) |
| 1851 | Thomas Draper |
| 1855 | Robert Richardson |
| 1859 | To let (*Lancaster Guardian*, 19/2/1859) |

Site demolished to give access to Mitchell's Brewery from Church Street
[Noted by Richard Bond as closed within his lifetime (1820–91)]

## Bee Hive (Beerhouse)　　　　　　　　　　　　　　　　　　　　Rose Street

(Is this the same as *Sawyers' Arms*?)

| | |
|---|---|
| 1851 | Agnes Bradley |
| 1881–86 | Charles Ralph (1881 census) |
| 1913 | R. Ralph |

(Some of the following Beerhouses probably had names and may be duplicated in the list of named inns below; in absence of other information they may be assumed to date from 1830 or later, resulting from the Beer Act.)

---

*Beerhouse*                                                    Spring Garden Street

James Tatham
[Noted by Richard Bond as closed within his lifetime (1820–91)]

---

*Beerhouse*                                                    China Street

Mrs Woodhouse
[Noted by Richard Bond as closed within his lifetime (1820–91)]

---

*Beerhouse*                                                    Edward Street

1820–74     C. Areston (W. King in Lancaster Inns & Public Houses folder)

---

*Beerhouse*                                                    Penny Street

1820–74     Septimus Brown (W. King in Lancaster Inns & Public Houses folder)

---

*Beerhouse*                                                    St George's Quay

1820–74     Mrs Waterhouse (W. King in Lancaster Inns & Public Houses folder)
1851        Thos Waterhouse

---

*Beerhouse*                                                    King Street

1820–74     Thomas Miller (W. King in Lancaster Inns & Public Houses folder)

---

*Beerhouse*                                                    Wood Street

1820–74     J. Steel (W. King in Lancaster Inns & Public Houses folder)

---

*Beerhouse*                                                    St Leonardgate

1820–74     Mrs Wadsworth (W. King in Lancaster Inns & Public Houses folder)

## *Beerhouse*                                            Bridge Lane

1820–74       Mrs Bond (W. King in Lancaster Inns & Public Houses folder)
(This may be the same as the *Three Mariners*)

## *Beerhouse* (see *James Harford*)                           Penny Street

1913         J. Harford

## *Bird In Hand*                                                   Skerton

1796–1844      John Longfield (LRO QSB3/132; QSB3/151; QSB3/160/5/1; QSB3/168/4/1)

## *Bird in Hand* (see *Wild Boar*)                             Penny Street

## *Black Bull* (now *Duke of Lancaster*)                   75 Church Street

This inn originally stood on the south side of Church Street, one door down from the junction with China Lane. It is first recorded in 1743. In 1794 Scarr's waggon left here every Friday for York, returning the same day (Universal British Directory). In 1825 the following carriers left from here: Edward Briggs for Burton in Kendal every Wednesday and Saturday, Thomas Parrington for Dent every Friday, Jeffry Metcalf for Kirkby Lonsdale every Wednesday and Saturday, Edward Carr for Milnthorpe every Tuesday and Saturday, Thomas Atkinson for Milnthorpe and Kendal every Tuesday and Saturday, and George Parrington for Myerscough every Saturday. (Baines' Directory) The building next door to the west was demolished as part of the general widening of China Lane c.1895 and in c.1907 the inn was rebuilt on the same site, now the corner with China Street, in a sort of free baroque, with a circular corner tower. In 1977 it was renamed *Duke of Lancaster*. It is one of the seven or so oldest inns in Lancaster, its site having been used continuously for over two hundred and sixty years.

1743–49       William Chippendale (Stallenge Rolls)
1778–86       Benjamin Mason (Stallenge Rolls; will in LRO, WRW/A 1787)
1786            Mrs Mason (Stallenge Rolls)
1787–94       Thomas Walton (Stallenge Rolls)
1806–9        Mark Irwin
1809–10       T. Waller
1822            J. Holden
1825            John Kitchen
1828            John Schofield
1834–39       Catherine Threlfall (For sale, *Lancaster Gazette*, 21/12/1839)
1842–51       William Masheder (Library Pamphlet Box S10)
1853            William McKie
1855            Mary Masheder
1864–65       William Hodgson (1865 Election petition)
1871–72       William Webster

| | |
|---|---|
| 1881 | Ann Webster |
| 1886–90 | William Hayhurst |
| 1896 | F. L. Bell |
| 1901 | F. Day |
| c1907 | Rebuilt on same site |
| 1913 | J. F. Barker |
| 1929 | ? |
| 1934 | John Reeday |
| 1956–57 | ? |
| 1977 | Renamed *Duke of Lancaster* |

*Black Bull/Duke of Lancaster*, Church Street.

## Black Bull (later *Skerton Hotel*)    2–4 Owen Road, Skerton

This inn stood on the east side of Owen Road, in Skerton, near the end of Skerton Bridge. It is recorded from 1815 until 1896, when it was extended southwards, and renamed the *Skerton Hotel*. A sale catalogue of 1917 is in the Library (Library S 1/68). A stained glass window of 1891 depicting Sir Richard Owen was taken out of this inn and given to the City Museum in the late 1980s.

| | |
|---|---|
| 1815–18 | Jonathan Tiffin (LRO QSB3/151) |
| 1822 | M. Tiffin |
| c1825 | Shown (Library plan PL 53/41) as *Bull Inn* on corner of main road with Main Street |
| 1823–36 | Richard Myerscough (QSB3/160/5/1; QSB3/168/4/1; will in LRO WRW/A 1836) |
| 1843–46 | Mrs Mary Masker or Myerscough (*Lancaster Gazette* 18/2/1843; will LRO WRW/A 1846) |
| 1851–53 | Ralph Gerrard (will LRO WRW/A 1853) |
| 1856 | Elizabeth Gerrard |
| 1871–72 | William Lamb |
| 1881–90 | Ann Lamb |
| 1896–1901 | T. Cornthwaite |

*Black Bull/Skerton Hotel*, Owen Road.

(Despite some inconsistency in recorded landlords and dates, this seems to have become or merged with the *Skerton Hotel* in 1896).

**Black Cat** (later *Athenaeum*)                                   95–7 St Leonardgate

(Also *Wilkinson's Vaults?*)

This inn stood on the south side of St Leonardgate, opposite Gillow's Works and near the Theatre, which had been renamed The Athenaeum in the mid-nineteenth century. It is first recorded in 1789–90 and deeds to the site are in the LRO (LRO MBLa Deeds (Acc 4797) Box 89) and among LCC Deeds (LCC Deeds 195/12). Its name was changed to *Athenaeum Hotel* from 1899. It was demolished, along with a great deal of other property on St Leonardgate in 1961 and its site is now a car park.

| | |
|---|---|
| 1789–90 | William Cooper (Stallenge Rolls) |
| 1794 | Eleanor Woods |
| 1818–22 | Mary Barber |
| 1825 | William Gardner |
| 1828 | James Parker |
| 1834–44 | Henry Bownell |
| 1851 | Jane Carter |
| 1852 | William Spencer |
| 1854 | William Barrow (*Lancaster Guardian*, 4/3/1854) |
| 1855 | John Waters |
| 1857–72 | James Townley (1865 Election petition) |
| 1881–95 | Henry Wilkinson (1881 census; 1895 Election petition) |
| 1896–1901 | W. Snape |

(later known as *Athenaeum Hotel* from 1899)

---

**Black Horse**                                             14 Common Garden Street

Stood on the north side of Common Garden Street, three doors east of the market entrance. It was owned by the Corporation (LCC Deeds 125/6). First recorded in 1793 it was from 1797–1852 the meeting place of the Philippi Club. This was a drinking club made up of the elite of the town, and its president wore a deep-crowned, broad-brimmed hat. (Cross Fleury, *Time-Honoured Lancaster*, 1891, 480–1) This hat and a punch ladle belonging to the club were exhibited at the Old Lancaster Exhibition in 1908. (Old Lancaster Exhibition, 1908, 51, 3) The inn was demolished in 1960 as part of a general rebuilding around the Market.

| | |
|---|---|
| 1793 | Owned by Corporation. Mrs Bradley (E. Kennerley; Library MS 8783) |
| 1794 | John Bradley |
| 1803 | Richard Singleton |
| 1818–56 | Agnes Starkie |
| 1864 | James Dunderdale |
| 1871–1913 | William Mitchell (1881 Census) |
| 1929 | ? |
| 1934 | L. Denton |
| 1956–57 | ? |
| 1960 | Demolished |

*Black Horse*                                                                 19 Main Street, Skerton

Stood on the west side of Main Street at its south end, in Hill's Court. Its deeds are in LCC.
(LCC Deeds 227/22) It survived from 1815 until after 1954.

| | |
|---|---|
| 1815–22 | Rachel Mawson (LRO QSB3/151) |
| 1844–65 | William Mather or Mathers (1865 Election petition) |
| 1871–72 | William Taylor |
| 1881 | Thomas Garner |
| 1886 | Matthew Battersby |
| 1889–90 | T. Liver |
| 1896–1901 | H. Hamilton |
| 1913 | D. Byron |
| 1929 | J. Coffey |
| 1934 | Richard Airey |

*(Black) Swan* (Beerhouse)                                                    133 St Leonardgate

| | |
|---|---|
| 1756–1844 | (E. Kennerley; Library MS 8783) |
| 1844 | Richard Howarth |
| 1864–65 | Mrs Elizabeth Ralph (1865 Election petition) |
| 1881 | (Census) John Ralph |
| 1886–1901 | Joseph Lloyd or Lloyds (1901 Census) |
| 1906 | Chief Constable objected to renewal of license (*Lancaster Guardian*, 3/3/1906) |

*Blazing Tub*                                                                  Church Street

| | |
|---|---|
| 1820–74 | (W. King in Lancaster Inns & Public Houses folder) |

[Noted by Richard Bond as closed within his lifetime (1820–91)]

*The Blob Shop* (formerly *The Borough Club*, now once more *The Borough*) Dalton Square

Recent

| | |
|---|---|
| 2006 | M. R. Horner |

**Blue Anchor** (now *1725* Tapas Bar)                    30 Market Street

This inn has stood in the north-east corner of Market Square since at least 1725 and if the existing building is this old, as it appears to be, then it may be the oldest building in Lancaster continuously used as an inn. Indeed, from its position in the Market Square this could even be a much older site, a prime candidate for a medieval inn, but so far lacking any documentary evidence to take it this far back. (LCC Deeds 65/15) In 1766 it had 18 windows taxed. It was extensively refurbished in 1990, but still retains a very similar appearance to that which it had over two and a half centuries ago.

| | |
|---|---|
| 1725 | (E. Kennerley; Library MS 8783) |
| 1726 | Robert Armstrong |
| 1750–62 | William Coward (son appears in Apprentice Rolls); will (LRO, WRW/A 1762) |
| 1766 | inn had 18 windows taxed (Kennerley, Library MS 8783) |
| 1775–85 | John Thorley (d. 1785, Lancaster PRs) |
| 1794 | Mary Thorley |
| 1803 | James Wilson |
| 1818–34 | Leonard Miller |
| 1844 | Richard Atkinson |
| 1851 | John Hodgson |
| 1856 | Thomas Stewart |
| 1859 | John McCann, lease for 7 years (Library MS 2432) |
| 1864–72 | Joseph Crook |
| 1881–90 | Edward Parkinson (1881 census) |
| 1896–1901 | J. H. Wilkinson |
| 1902 | J. Day |
| 1913 | W. Leighton |
| 1929–34 | Robert Kew |
| 1956–57 | ? |
| 1970 | ? |
| 2003 | G. Moody and E. J. Ramsay |
| 2005 | P. Ward and G. Taylor |
| 2006 | Mitchell's of Lancaster (Brewers) Ltd. |
| 2007 | Refitted and became 1725 Tapas Bar |

*Blue Anchor/1725 Tapas Bar*, Market Square.

## Blue Anchor                                          75 Main Street, Skerton

This inn has stood on the west side of Main Street, now Mainway, Skerton, since 1815. The present building, in a contemporary style, replaced the original on the same site in 1959, at a time when Skerton was being almost wholly remodelled, with the loss of the Ramparts, the old Main Street and Captains' Row.

| | |
|---|---|
| 1815–17 | Richard Nuttall (LRO QSB3/151; sale for creditors; Library Scrapbook 6, 30) |
| 1822 | G. R. Hewetson |
| 1823–34 | Richard Warbrick jnr (LRO QSB3/160/5/1; QSB3/168/4/1) |
| 1844–49 | William Smith (will LRO WRW/A 1849) |
| 1851–56 | Nicholas Drinkall |
| 1871–72 | Elizabeth Cowell |
| 1881 | Thomas Smith |
| 1886–90 | Richard Townley |
| 1895–1901 | John Robinson (1895 Election petition) |
| 1913 | G. H. Procter |
| 1929 | I. W. Burrow |
| 1934 | A. Garnett |
| 1956–57 | ? |
| 1959 | Demolished and rebuilt on same site |
| 2003 | Closed. Now a shop |

*Blue Anchor*, Skerton.

## Blue Anchor                                          15 St George's Quay

This inn stood on St George's Quay, to the south east of Oak Street, from at least 1761, when it is recorded as 'late Henry Langton, mariner', until its demolition in 1963.

| | |
|---|---|
| 1761 | Late Henry Langton, mariner (E. Kennerley; Library MS 8783) |
| 1818–28 | George Warbrick |

| | |
|---|---|
| 1834 | James Rigg Berry |
| 1840 | William Brockbank, innkeeper and sailmaker, will (LRO WRW/A 1840) |
| 1844–56 | Agnes Brockbank |
| 1864 | Thomas Hodgson |
| 1865 | Miss Hodgson (Election Petition) |
| 1871–72 | Robert Darbyshire |
| 1881 | Joseph Ellinson |
| 1886–96 | Thomas Moore |
| 1901 | Mrs B. Parkinson |
| 1913 | W. Watson |
| 1929 | W. T. Jackson |
| 1934 | A. J. Harfield |
| 1963 | Demolished |

## Blue Bell ?

| | |
|---|---|
| 1745 | Mrs Jackson (Stallenge Rolls) |

## Blue Bell (Beerhouse) 14 St George's Quay

| | |
|---|---|
| 1752–1891 | Deeds (LRO MBLa Deeds (Acc 4797) Box 88) |
| 1820–74 | Thomas Dixon (W. King in Lancaster Inns & Public Houses folder) |
| 1851 | Henry Dixon |
| 1865–81 | Mrs Agnes Dixon (1865 Election Petition; conveyance, Library MS 1437) |
| 1886 | Isaac Jackson |
| 1889–90 | J. R. Jackson |
| 1896 | J. Muckle |
| 1901 | J. Parkinson |
| 1906 | Chief Constable objected to renewal of license (*Lancaster Guardian*, 3/3/1906) |

## Blue Boar ?

(Possibly mistake for another 'Blue' name)

| | |
|---|---|
| 1895 | (Election petition) |

## Blue Stoops Market Street

| | |
|---|---|
| 1717–45 | (E. Kennerley; Library MS 8783) |
| 1715 | 21 year lease, part of the estate of the late William Penny (Library MS 2163) |
| 1746 | John Walker (Library MS 2462) |

*Boar's Head*                                                                                          Bridge Lane

1794          Joseph Fallows


*Boar's Head*                                                                                 26 St Nicholas Street

This inn stood in St Nicholas Street from about 1786 until its demolition as part of the St
Nicholas Centre redevelopment in 1967–70. The name was then transferred to a new site nearby
in Great John Street until it was tastelessly renamed *Ruxton's* in about 2002, after the doctor
who murdered his wife and maid nearby in Dalton Square in 1935, being again renamed *The
Square* in 2006.

| | |
|---|---|
| 1786–95 | Thomas Edmondson (Stallenge Rolls) |
| 1794 | John Edmondson |
| 1796 | Thomas Edmondson (Library MS 3706) |
| 1801 | Joseph Wilkinson |
| 1809–29 | G. Satterthwaite |
| 1834–51 | Thomas Satterthwaite |
| 1855 | William Townson |
| 1864–81 | Joseph Dowthwaite (1881 Census) |
| 1886 | Henry Redwood |
| 1889–90 | J. W. Batty |
| 1895–96 | ex-Inspector R. Parkinson (1895 Election petition) |
| 1901 | William McIntosh, manager (1901 census) |
| 1913 | J. Tyson |
| 1929–34 | H. Heading |
| 1956–57 | ? |
| *c.*1967 | Demolished in redevelopment |


*Boar's Head* (then *Ruxton's*, now *The Square*)                                Great John Street

(rebuilt on new site after building of St Nicholas Centre, *c.*1967–70)

| | |
|---|---|
| 1970 | H. Tyrer |
| 2003 | ? |
| 2006 | Inns & Leisure Ltd. |


*Bobbin* (see *Midland* and *Priory*)                                                       Cable Street

| | |
|---|---|
| 2003 | D. P. Barlow and E. J. Ramsay |
| 2006 | Mitchell's of Lancaster (Brewers) Ltd. |


*Boot & Shoe*                                                                                            Skerton

1820–74       M. Miller (W. King in Lancaster Inns & Public Houses folder)

**Boot & Shoe**                                               Scotforth Road, Scotforth

This is one of the two inns in Scotforth which have survived since it was a village detached
from Lancaster by open country. It dates from *c.*1799 and stands on the east side of the turn-
pike road (the modern A6). It belonged to the Trustees of Penny's and Heysham's Charities,
according to nineteenth-century documents in Lancaster Library (Library MSS 8096, 8109,
1348) A sale catalogue of 1898 also survives (Library S 1/32).

| | |
|---|---|
| 1799–1828 | Richard Dixon or Dickson (LRO QSB3/151; QSB3/160/5/1; QSB3/168/4/1) |
| 1852 | John Wilkinson, will (LRO WRW/A 1852) |
| 1852–54 | Ann Wilkinson |
| 1865–81 | William Jackson (1865 Election Petition) |
| 1884 | George Mansergh, lease for 5 years (Library MS 1348) |
| 1898 | Sale catalogue (Library S 1/32) |
| 1901–13 | W. Proctor |
| 1929–34 | R. Mashiter |
| 1956–57 | ? |
| 2006 | Mitchell's of Lancaster (Brewers) Ltd. |

*Boot & Shoe*, Scotforth.

**Boot & Shoe**                                                             Cheapside

This inn stood in Market Street at the corner of Cheapside from 1772 until about 1857. It is one
of those noted by Richard Bond as having closed within his lifetime (1820–91).

| | |
|---|---|
| 1772 | Simeon Dodgson (Egerton MS, John Rylands Library) |
| 1782–90 | James Townson (Stallenge Rolls) |
| 1792 | Richard Lancaster (Stallenge Rolls) |
| 1794 | Robert Parkinson |
| 1808 | Gawen Heaton |
| 1818–25 | William Newton. Auction (Library Scrapbook 3, 20) |
| 1828–32 | Thomas Williamson, will (LRO WRW/A 1832) |
| 1834–44 | Richard Hadwen |
| 1851 | John Kitchen |
| –1855 | Thomas Kew |
| 1855 | William Hollows |
| 1856 | Thomas Hogarth |
| 1857 | Robert Hornby |

## Boundary Inn
30 South Road, Greaves

| 1866 | Mentioned in evidence for Scotforth Murder |
|------|---------------------------------------------|
| 1871–72 | Richard Batty |
| 1881 | J. Jackson |
| 1886–90 | Robert Wolfenden |
| 1896 | M. R. Russel |
| 1901 | R. H. Banks |
| 1913 | W. Hunter |
| 1929 | ? |
| 1934 | A. Gardner |
| 1956–57 | ? |
| 1970 | R. W. Brown |
| 1970 | Demolished for new roundabout |

Former *Boundary Inn* at the Pointer, demolished 1970 and now replaced by a big roundabout. (Courtesy of Lancaster City Museum part of Lancashire Museums)

## Bowerham Hotel
Gordon Terrace, Bowerham Road

| c.1901 | Opened |
|--------|--------|
| 1911–34 | Benjamin Robert Procter |
| 1956–57 | ? |
| 2006 | Mitchell's of Lancaster (Brewers) Ltd. |

*Bowerham Hotel*, Bowerham.

**Bowling Green**                                          Scotforth Road, Scotforth

This, the other old inn of Scotforth (see *Boot & Shoe*) is first recorded in 1815. It was demolished in 1981 and rebuilt on a new site nearby.

| | |
|---|---|
| 1815 | Timothy Longton (LRO QSB3/151) |
| 1823–56 | John Griffin (LRO QSB3/160/5/1; QSB3/168/4/1) |
| 1865 | William Jackson (Election petition) |
| 1871–72 | Alice Coates |
| 1881 | Thomas Dearden |
| 1901–06 | S. Carey |
| 1913–34 | J. Parker |
| 1956–57 | ? |
| 1981 | Demolished and rebuilt on new site |

---

**Bowling Green**                                          Scotforth Road, Scotforth

2006        D. G. I. Lawson and A. Lawson

Bowling Green, Scotforth.

---

**Bowling Green**                                                             ?

1754        Henry Geldart (Stallenge Rolls)

---

**Bowling Green**                                          Meeting House Lane

(This may in fact record the clubhouse of the bowling green which stood there).

1851        Benjamin Hartley

---

**Brewery (New)**                                          Bryer Street

1809        Martha Horner, sale (*Lancaster Gazette*, 24/8/1809)
[Noted by Richard Bond as closed within his lifetime (1820–91)]

## Bridge Inn                                                      Parliament Street

Housed in the eyecatching range of buildings constructed by Thomas Harrison at the Lancaster end of Skerton Bridge, this inn doubled as a toll-house, where tolls were exacted upon goods passing through. It stands on Parliament Street and although the buildings just about survive, the inn closed in about 1856 and became a private house. It is first recorded as an inn in 1787, when it was built.

It is noted by Richard Bond as having been closed within his lifetime (1820–91). The Bond family subsequently lived here. After many years of neglect the building has been refurbished as part of a wider redevelopment of the area (2005–6).

Former *Bridge Inn*, Parliament Street.

| | |
|---|---|
| 1787 | R. Dunderdale |
| 1794 | John Martin |
| 1803–14 | Robert Mansergh (*Lancaster Gazette*, 26/8/1807; will (LRO WRW/A 1814) |
| 1818–25 | Robert Atkinson |
| 1819 | Inn and tolls to be let for 7 years (Library S10) |
| 1828 | R. Warbreck |
| 1834–44 | Hugh Roades |
| 1851–56 | John Dobson |

[Noted by Richard Bond as closed within his lifetime (1820–91)]

---

## Britannia (Beerhouse)                                           Ullswater Road

A beerhouse on the east side of Ullswater Road (historically spelt Ulleswater), on the corner with Moor Lane, and first recorded in 1871, this is one of three inns on the Freehold estate, the roads of which are distinguished by their Lake District names.

| | |
|---|---|
| 1871–72 | William Iles |
| 1881–90 | John Shaw (1881 census) |
| 1896 | Mrs M. I. Hayton |
| 1901 | Mrs M. I. Murphy |
| 1901 | (Census) James Murphy |
| 1913 | W. Cornthwaite |
| 1929 | ? |
| 1934 | R. Cornthwaite |
| 1956–57 | ? |
| 1970 | L. Appleby |
| 2003 | P. Kennington |
| 2006 | R. C. Dow |

*Britannia*, Ullswater Road.

**British Queen**                                                    Wood Street

1864          Ann Dixon

---

**Brown Cow** (Beerhouse)                                      44 Penny Street

(see also *James Harford*)
This inn, originally a beerhouse, on the west side
of Penny Street, is first recorded in 1849. It was
overhauled and extended into the adjacent half of
the building in 2003–4.

1849          (E. Kennerley; Library MS 8783)
1881          Frederick K. Cornforth
1886–1901     John Whittam (1895 Election Petition)
1929          ?
1934          Mary A. Hulme
?             D. C. Gethin (still over door in 2003)
2006          N. Dunne

*Brown Cow*, Penny Street.

---

**Brown Cow**                                                   Market Street

1748-         (E. Kennerley; Library MS 8783)

---

**Bull's Head**                                                    Cheapside

Said to have been replaced by *Green Dragon*, but these were clearly in existence at the same
time (J. R. Spalding, Notes in Library)

1745          (E. Kennerley; Library MS 8783)
1767          J. Atkinson (Stallenge Rolls)
1772–77       James Vicars (Egerton MS, John Rylands Library; will (LRO WRW/A 1777)
1794          John Bells
1807–18       Robert Cartmell (handbill, Lancaster Central Library)
[Noted by Richard Bond as closed within his lifetime (1820–91)]
[The 'Bull's Head' itself was a piece of weathered limestone which stood over the door, itself
having a lintel dated 1678, up a yard off the west side of Cheapside, demolished 1984. The stone
is now in the City Museum.]

### Butchers' Arms (later *Bull's Head*) (Beerhouse) — 18 Common Garden Street

This beerhouse, which stood on the north side of Common Garden Street, on one corner of the Market entrance and adjacent to the *Black Horse* (qv), may have been known as the *Butchers' Arms* before 1857. (LCC Deeds 125/5) It was demolished in 1959 as part of the redevelopment of the area around the Market.

| | |
|---|---|
| pre 1857 | Known as Butchers' Arms (J. R. Spalding, Notes in Library) |
| 1865 | Edward Robinson (Election Petition) |
| 1881 | (Census) William Davis |
| 1886–1901 | George W. Milner |
| 1929 | ? |
| 1934 | John Martin |
| 1956–57 | ? |
| 1959 | Demolished |

### Cabinet Makers' Arms (Beerhouse) — 129 St Leonardgate

| | |
|---|---|
| 1865 | George Lund (Election petition) |
| 1881 | (Census) Mary Lund |
| 1886 | John Johnson |
| 1889–90 | J. N. Taylor |

Gone before 1900

### Cable Street Vaults — 42 Cable Street

| | |
|---|---|
| 1861–63 | Wilton Wood (Rate Books) |
| 1863–76 | Mary Wood (Rate Books) |
| 1886 | Richard Taylor |
| 1881–1901 | John Allen (Rate Books) |
| 1962 | Demolished |

### Carpenters' Arms (now *Three Mariners*) — 32 Bridge Lane

This ancient inn stands on what was the west side of Bridge Lane, but since 1939 and the re-routing of roads for the bus station, it has been the only building to preserve the old road line. It is first recorded in 1778. It was largely reroofed and refronted in 1961 when the front began to bulge outwards. Since 1986 it has been renamed *Three Mariners*, although the original site of that inn (qv) was elsewhere. It was famous for lacking cellars, the beer being kept in the attic because of the high water table.

| | |
|---|---|
| 1778 | Matthew Geldart (Stallenge Rolls) |
| 1778–83 | Benjamin Whiteside, son apprenticed (Apprentice Rolls; Stallenge Rolls) |
| 1818 | Agnes Bee |
| 1822–25 | Robert Baxter |
| 1828 | John Dunkley |
| 1834 | Thomas Wilson |

| 1844 | Joseph Dickinson |
| 1851 | Charles Swithenbank |
| 1851–72 | James Ellershaw (1865 Election Petition) |
| 1881 | (Census) Sarah Chippindale |
| 1886–90 | William L. Jackson |
| 1896 | William S. Jackson |
| 1901 | R. Knowles |
| 1913 | E. Hardy |
| 1934 | Richard Hayton |
| 1956–57 | ? |
| 1958- | J. Jones |
| 1970 | J. Knill Jones |
| 1986 | Renamed *Three Mariners* |

*Carpenters' Arms*, Bridge Lane in the 1920s. (Lancaster Library)
*Three Mariners*, Bridge Lane.

## Carpenters' Arms                                                    Skerton

| 1818–34 | Richard Waidson or Wadeson (LRO QSB3/160/5/1; QSB3/168/4/1) |
| 1835 | License not renewed |

## Carters' Arms (Beerhouse)                                  St George's Quay

| 1851 | Arthur Kirkham |

**Castle Hotel** (formerly **Bay Horse**, then **Kampus**, now **The Pub**)          China Street

(Rebuilt under new name after demolition of **Bay Horse** on same site)

| | |
|---|---|
| 1901 | C. Lawton |
| 1913 | W. Rainbird |
| 1929 | ? |
| 1934 | Sarah M. Rainbird |
| 1956–57 | ? |
| 1970 | J. H. Potts |
| 1994–95 | Matt Jackson |
| 2003 | ? |
| 2004 | Renamed *Kampus* |
| 2006 | Renamed *The Pub* |
| 2006 | D. R. M. Pegram |

---

**Cattle Market Tavern**          Mary Street

| | |
|---|---|
| 1820–74 | R. Brotherton (W. King in Lancaster Inns & Public Houses folder) |

---

**Chicago Rock**          New Street

Recent

---

**Coach & Six**          ?

| | |
|---|---|
| 1754–60 | James Jackson (Stallenge Rolls; Militia Ballot List; probate inventory (LRO WRW/A 1760) |

---

**Coach & Horses**          China Lane

Acted as bar for *Feathers Inn*, which had none of its own.

| | |
|---|---|
| 1756 | (E. Kennerley; Library MS 8783) |
| 1818 | John Nixon |
| 1822 | W. Greenall |
| 1825–34 | Christopher Hinde. Sale of inn and houses 31/3/1826 (Library Scrapbook 3, 46) |
| 1896 | Demolished |

---

**Coach Makers' Arms** (Beerhouse)          91 St Leonardgate

| | |
|---|---|
| 1881 | (Census) James Park |
| 1886–90 | Christopher Foster |
| 1896–1901 | W. Snape |
| 1906 | Chief Constable objected to renewal of license (*Lancaster Guardian*, 3/3/1906) |

**Cock**                                                                                         North Road

Predecessor to *Ship Inn*, see also *Three Squirrels*
(Cross Fleury, *Time-Honoured Lancaster*, 454)


**Cockpit Inn**                                                                                King Street

(J. R. Spalding, Notes in Library)


**Commercial Inn**                                                                          Market Street

This large inn stood on the north side of Market Square, where the easternmost part of the Library
now stands. It replaced 'Mr Hornby's Great House', which is known from the deeds (LCC Deeds
85/3) and a watercolour drawing of *c.*1770 now in the Whitworth Art Gallery, Manchester, and
stood next to the **Royal Oak**. It was built *c.*1799 and is first recorded as an inn in 1803. In 1825 the
following carriers left from here: Thomas Holme every Saturday for Leck, Robert Hodgson every
Saturday for Preston Patrick, and Mary Willan every Saturday for Tunstall. It ceased to function
in 1890, when Joseph Sly sold it to Lancaster Corporation. It was taken over for use by the police
and fire brigade, the latter using the old inn yard for storage of the fire engine, ladders and hoses.
The building itself was demolished in 1932 for the building of the Library.

| | |
|---|---|
| 1803 | Mr Miller |
| 1805 | J. Wilson (*Lancaster Gazette*, 25/5/05) |
| (1806 | (Kennerley, Library MS 8783) |
| 1809–17 | John Wilson (*Lancaster Gazette*, 2/6/1810) |
| 1818–21 | Mrs Hannah Wilson |
| 1821 | Notice to creditors of late Mrs Hannah Wilson (Library Scrapbook 6, pt 2, 40v; |
| | Sale notice, *Lancaster Gazette*, 23/6/1821) |
| 1822 | I. Pritt |
| 1825 | George Watson |
| 1828–36 | John Bagot or Baggot |
| 1838 | Mrs Lough |
| 1844 | Ann Marsh? |
| 1851 | George Riley |
| –1854 | Mary Baxter |
| 1854 | James Dugdale |
| 1856 | John Baxter |
| 1864–65 | Henry Richmond (1865 Election Petition) |
| 1871–72 | Richard Jackson |
| 1881 | (Census) William Clark |
| 1886–90 | Thomas Soar |
| 1890 | Sold for use as Police and Fire Station |


**Cordwainers' Arms** (Beerhouse)                                                      Marton Street

1851      George Hodgson
Went out of existence during the nineteenth century (J. R. Spalding, Notes in Library)

## Corporation Arms

124 Penny Street

This ancient inn stood on the west side of what was then Penny Street, but now King Street, just north of the *White Cross* (qv). It was a simple two-storey, early eighteenth-century building, with an elaborate carved stone version of the arms of Lancaster above its door, now in the City Museum. It is first recorded in 1781. In 1825 the carrier John Taylor left here every alternate Monday for Kirkby Lonsdale. At the end of the nineteenth century, alterations to improve the southern approach to the town led to much demolition in this area. Sale catalogues for 1899 and 1901 are in the Library (Library S 1/41) and the inn was demolished in 1901. Its name was briefly transferred to a new inn a little to the south east, the *Corporation Hotel*, which quickly changed its name to the *Alexandra* (qv).

Photograph of the **Corporation Arms** and to its left the old **White Cross**, before this part of Penny Street was demolished and rebuilt in about 1900. (Courtesy of Lancaster City Museum part of Lancashire Museums)

| | |
|---|---|
| 1781 | (E. Kennerley; Library MS 8783) |
| 1781 | W. Bond/J. Forder |
| 1814–15 | Nicholas Robinson |
| 1818–25 | Jane Mansergh |
| 1828 | James Riley |
| 1834 | William Parker |
| 1844 | Henry Row |
| 1851 | Richard Bradley |
| 1855 | Hannah Row |
| 1857–64 | Thomas Dearden |
| 1871–72 | John Myers |
| 1881 | (Census) James Farnworth |
| 1886–90 | Mrs Margaret Farnworth or Farnswood |
| c1890 | Photo shows Edward Hodgkinson |
| 1896 | Mrs E. Hodgkinson |
| 1899 | Sale catalogue (Library S 1/41) |
| 1901 | Demolished |

## Corporation Hotel (later *Alexandra Hotel*)

Penny Street

(The new hotel of *c*.1901–2 was briefly titled thus)
| | |
|---|---|
| 1913 | W. D. Jackson |

## County Hotel

Station Road

| | |
|---|---|
| 1871–86 | Samuel Ducksbury (1881 Census) |
| 1901 | C. E. Ducksbury |
| 1913 | J. S. Ducksbury |
| 1929 | W. S. Spencer |
| 1934 | T. R. Blackhurst |
| 1956–57 | ? |
| 1970 | J. Blades |

## Craven Heifer Inn (Beerhouse)                                        North Road

1807–12    Date of original Craven Heifer, so likely date of inn
1811–20    James Howson (Rule Book 1784–1822, f.111)
1864–65    Samuel Dobson (1865 Election Petition)
[Noted by Richard Bond as closed within his lifetime (1820–91)]


## Crooked Billet                                                        Church Street

1765       (E. Kennerley; Library MS 8783)
1790–94    Thomas Parkinson (Stallenge Rolls)
1855       Advertised to let
[Noted by Richard Bond as closed within his lifetime (1820–91)]


## Cross Keys                                                            9 Market Street

This ancient inn lay on the south side of Market Street, five doors up from Horseshoe Corner.
It was a seventeenth-century building with carved dates of 1613 and 1625, the latter over the
kitchen doorway. There was also a carved panel reading GT 1629, the initials standing for George
Toulnson or Townson. Whether it was an inn this early is uncertain, and we cannot prove its
existence as one until 1720, with a Probate Inventory of Henry Hodgson. In 1794 Atkinson's
waggon left here every Wednesday for York, returning on the Tuesday (Universal British
Directory). A handbill for the inn under D. Bell in 1805 is in the Soulby Collection at Barrow
in Furness. In 1825 the following carriers left from here: Thomas Preston for Pilling every
Saturday and James Brunton for Yealand every Tuesday and Saturday. (Baines' *Directory*) The
inn is last recorded in 1970, when it was demolished and its site used for the new store of Bhs.

1652       owner George Toulnson JP (Cross Fleury, *Time-Honoured Lancaster*, 1891, 453)
1720       Probate inventory of Henry Hodgson (LRO WRW/A 1720)
1756       Thomas Warbreck (Stallenge Rolls)
1762       Henry Whiteside (Stallenge Rolls)
1765       Thomas Warbrick (Hewitson, Memoranda, 90)
1772       Henry Whiteside (Egerton MS, John Rylands Library)
1787       John Whiteside (Hewitson, Memoranda, 116)
1794–1805  John Bell (Library MS 3706; will (LRO WRW/A 1805)
1805       D. Bell (female) (CRO Soulby Coll., ZS45)
1808       Moses Aaron James Gurney (Rule Book 1784–1822, f.96ff)
?          James Foster
1812       Advert for sale (*Lancaster Gazette*, 29/8/1812)
1818–44    Thomas Gardiner or Gardner
1851       Jerrimiah Parkinson
1853       Margaret Brown
1858–7?    William Bullfield, husband of above (1865 Election Petition)
?          William Smith, second husband of Margaret Brown
1881       J. T. Railton?
1881       (Census) Margaret Smith
1886–90    Samuel Ducksbury

| ? | John Beatson Lawson |
| 1896–1901 | Thomas Gribbin |
| ? | William Lancaster |
| ? | George Frederick Hoggarth |
| 1913 | Alfred Clowes |
| 1929 | ? |
| 1934 | T. Parkin |
| 1956–57 | ? |
| 1970 | J. E. Williams |

Demolished and site used for British Home Stores

---

## *Crown* (Beerhouse)             18 St Leonardgate

This beerhouse, standing on the north side of St Leonardgate, near its east end, is first
recorded in 1881. It originally occupied one of a pair of mid-Georgian houses, but later spread
into the neighbouring part. It ceased to be used in the 1990s and has been derelict for many
years.

| ? | Dickinson |
| ? | Mary Ellen Dickinson |
| 1854 | Advertised to let |
| 1865 | Richard Batty (Election petition) |
| 1881–90 | Joshua Hall (1881 census) |
| 1896 | Mrs E. Turner |
| 1901–13 | John Herbert (1901 census) |
| 1929 | ? |
| 1934 | Isabella Herbert |
| 1956–57 | ? |
| 1970 | A. Herbert |

(Has stood derelict since closure
c.1995)

Former *Crown*, St Leonardgate.

---

## *Crown & Mitre*             Common Garden Street

| 1794 | James Topham |
| 1804 | George Metcalfe (*Lancaster Gazette*, 23/8/1804) |
| 1818 | (J. R. Spalding, Notes in Library) |

---

## *Crowther Arms*             St Leonardgate

| 1929 | ? |

## Custom House Tavern                                                  St George's Quay

| | |
|---|---|
| 1818–22 | W. Mecoid |
| 1825–34 | Margaret Mecoid |
| 1844 | Mary Gardner |
| 1851 | Thomas Helme |
| 1856 | John Bland |
| 1864 | Ann Wilkinson |
| 1865 | Halliday (Election Petition) |
| 1870 | Application for new license refused? (*Lancaster Guardian*, 27/8/1870) |

[Noted by Richard Bond as closed within his lifetime (1820–91)]

## Dales Vaults (see *Rose & Crown* or *Tubs*)                        James Street

## Dalton Arms (see *Mechanics' Arms*) (Beerhouse)            26 Parliament Street

There seems some overlap with the *Mechanics' Arms*, so there is some doubt about their identity. Richard Bond's statement also complicates the issue.

| | |
|---|---|
| 1820 | J. Warbrick |
| –1844 | Richard Warbrick, will (LRO WRW/A 1844) |
| 1851 | Jane Warbrick |
| 1856 | John Carr |
| 1864–65 | John Bradley (1865 Election Petition) |
| 1871–72 | Alice Bradley |
| 1889–90 | J. Marshall |
| 1896–1901 | Henry Hayes |
| 1901 | (Census) It seems to be a lodging house, not an inn, at this date. |

[Noted by Richard Bond as closed within his lifetime (1820–91)]

## Dog & Partridge                                                      China Lane

| | |
|---|---|
| 1794 | Robert Warbrick |

## Dog & Partridge                                                   Damside Street

| | |
|---|---|
| 1853 | G. Croskill (*Lancaster Gazette*, 9/5/1853) |

(J. R. Spalding, Notes in Library)

## Dolphin (Old)                                          Bridge Lane

| | |
|---|---|
| 1782 | William Taylor (Stallenge Rolls) |
| 1783 | Jonathan Winder (Stallenge Rolls) |
| 1784–85 | Robert Wright (Stallenge Rolls) |
| 1790 | John Garth (Stallenge Rolls) |

## Dolphin                                                        Chapel Street

| | |
|---|---|
| 1754 | (E. Kennerley; Library MS 8783) |
| 1794 | John Sharples |
| 1818–34 | Agnes Russell |
| 1844–65 | James Rowe (1865 Election Petition) |

[Noted by Richard Bond as closed within his lifetime (1820–91)]

## Duke of Cumberland (Head)                                  Market Street

Such a name is likely to have originated in 1745–46, in the aftermath of the Jacobite revolt and its suppression.

| | |
|---|---|
| 1750–53 | (E. Kennerley; Library MS 8783) |
| 1750 | Robert Berry |
| 1779–86 | Giles Townson (Stallenge Rolls) |

## Duke of Lancaster (see Black Bull)                            75 Church Street

| | |
|---|---|
| 1977 | Renamed from Black Bull |
| 2003 | J. Ball |
| 2006 | Mitchell's of Lancaster (Brewers) Ltd. |

## Durham Ox                                                Wood Street

| | |
|---|---|
| c.1801–10 | Date of original Durham Ox, so likely date of inn |

[Noted by Richard Bond as closed within his lifetime (1820–91)]

## Dwarf                                                           Skerton

| | |
|---|---|
| 1820–74 | Miss Savage (W. King in Lancaster Inns & Public Houses folder) |

### Eagle & Child
Market Street

| | |
|---|---|
| 1713 | (E. Kennerley; Library MS 8783) |
| –1713 | Robert Marshall |
| 1717 | 'burgage on south side of Market Street called the Eagle & Child' (LRO, DDL 718) |

### Edwardian (formerly *King Edward VII*, later *Edwards*, then *Muse*, now *LAOne*)
Penny Street

(Perhaps also originally *Stonemasons' Arms*, then *Kelsall's Vaults*)

| | |
|---|---|
| 2003 | I. J. Huntington |
| 2006 | L. C. Miller and W. A. Gardner |

*Edwardian/LAOne*, Penny Street.

### Ellershaw's Arms
Skerton

| | |
|---|---|
| 1820–74 | Mrs Ellershaw (W. King in Lancaster Inns & Public Houses folder) |

### Farmers' Arms (formerly *White Cross*, now *Penny Street Bridge*)
Penny Street

| | |
|---|---|
| 1913 | W. J. Williams |
| 1929 | ? |
| 1934 | William J. Watson |
| 1956–57 | ? |
| 1970 | C. E. Phillips |
| 2003 | A. R. Williams |

### Fat Scot (Scotsman) (renamed Spooners, now Mood)                    17 Mary Street

This beerhouse, in Mary Street, on the corner of Gage Street, is first recorded in 1844. A converted Georgian warehouse it occupies part of the range of backbuildings and warehouses associated with the late eighteenth-century development of Dalton Square (this forms the rear of Lot 17 originally apportioned in 1784). It was renamed *Spooners* after an extensive refit in about 2000 and became *Mood* in 2004.

| | |
|---|---|
| 1844 | Thomas Carter |
| 1851 | Henry Hargreaves |
| −1854 | Robert Bratherton |
| 1854 | Peter Moore |
| 1864 | William Jackson |
| 1865 | John Forrest (Election petition) |
| 1871–72 | Ambrose Worthington |
| 1881 | (Census) William Stockdale |
| 1886 | William Billington |
| 1889–90 | A. Smallshaw |
| 1896 | J. Briscoe |
| 1901 | F. L. Bell |
| 1913 | Francis Riley |
| 1929 | ? |
| 1934 | Edward Reddin |
| 1956–57 | ? |
| 1970 | G. Anderson |
| 2006 | Mitchell's of Lancaster (Brewers) Ltd. |

*Fat Scot/Mood*, Mary Street.

### Feathers Hotel                    60 Market Street

(Used *Coach & Horses* as public bar)

| | |
|---|---|
| 1820 | C. Hind (J. R. Spalding, Notes in Library) |
| 1844 | Joseph Sly |
| 1851–56 | Mary Ann Bell |
| 1864 | John Huntington |
| 1871–72 | John Fisher |
| 1881–86 | John T. Railton (1881 census) |
| 1889–90 | W. Rainbird |

Closed 1895 and license transferred to Moorlands Hotel

### Fibber Magee's (formerly Slip Inn)                    James Street

| | |
|---|---|
| 2006 | Mitchell's of Lancaster (Brewers) Ltd. |

## Foresters' Arms
Penny Street

1855          Advertised to let
1859          *Lancaster Guardian,* 23/7/1859
[Noted by Richard Bond as closed within his lifetime (1820–91)]

## Fox & Dogg
?

1722–23     (*The Rake's Diary; Journal of George Hilton,* 71; '... got into a pimping ale house calld the Fox & Dogg ...')

## Fox & Goose
Church Street

–1744       The house immediately west of the *Horse & Farrier* appears in deeds of 1744 as 'formerly known as Hordman's House or the *Fox & Goose,* in occupation of Robert Richardson'. (LCC Deeds 51/3)

## Fox & Goose
23 Queen Street

This inn was set up within what was a residential area, on the east side of Queen Street, on its corner with Ann Street. (LCC Deeds 141/12). It is first recorded in 1809. Perhaps its clientele, like that of the *Spinners' Arms,* was associated with Queen's Mill in Aldcliffe Lane? A sale catalogue of 1886 is in the Library (Library S 1/18). In 1964 the inn was demolished, and its licence transferred to a new inn in Newlands Road, Bowerham.

1809          (E. Kennerley; Library MS 8783)
1825          Thomas Camm
1828          James Robinson
1834          John Townson
1844          John Carson
1851          William Spencer
–1855       John Slater
1855          Peter Osbaldestone
1856          Joseph Gray
1864          Thomas Houghton
1865          John Foxcroft (Election Petition)
1871–72     Nancy Jackson
1881          David Gill
1886          Sale catalogue (Library S 1/18)
1886–90     Robert Miller
1895–1913   Thomas S. Hunter (1895 Election Petition)
1929          ?
1934          J.W. Reddin
1956–57     ?
1964          Demolished, license transferred to new inn of same name at Bowerham

## Fox & Goose

Newlands Road, Bowerham

| | |
|---|---|
| 1964 | License transferred from Queen Street inn of same name |
| 2006 | Mitchell's of Lancaster (Brewers) Ltd. |

## Freeholders' Arms (Beerhouse)

49 Ullswater Road

This beerhouse stands on the east side of Ullswater Rd, near the corner with Dalton Road. It is one of the three inns on the Freehold estate (see *Britannia* and *Rose Tavern*). The *Rose* and *Freeholders'* make their appearance in 1865, when they were used for 'treating' Liberal voters, not surprising considering the purpose of the estate. This had been created to boost the Liberal vote in the 1850s, by encouraging Liberal supporters to acquire sufficient land value to obtain the vote. The large size of the plots on this estate are the main legacy of the movement.

| | |
|---|---|
| 1865 | Richard Walsh (Election Petition) |
| 1871–72 | Allen Haythornthwaite |
| 1881 | (Census) John Atkinson |
| 1886–90 | Elizabeth Atkinson |
| 1896 | J. Thompson |
| 1901–13 | Mrs Ellen Bella Liver (1901 census) |
| 1929 | ? |
| 1934 | T. Collinson |
| 1956–57 | ? |
| 2003 | Sandra<br>E. Woof |
| 2006 | Inns &<br>Leisure Ltd. |

*Freeholders' Arms*, Ullswater Road.

*Friary* (formerly *Friary & Firkin*)                    Rosemary Lane/St Leonardgate

(Recent, converted from former Centenary Chapel)
2003        K. Gaskell
2006        Mitchells & Butlers Leisure Retail Ltd.

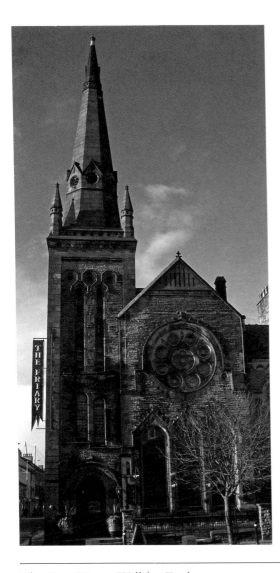

*Friary*, Rosemary Lane.

---

*The Gate Hangs Well* (or *Free*)                                        Skerton

1820–74     C. Knowles (W. King in Lancaster Inns & Public Houses folder) (Hewitson,
            Memoranda, 235, quotes verse on sign; 'This gate hangs well, and hinders none/
            Refresh and pay and travel on')
1851        'Inn abolished forty years ago' (1891) (Cross Fleury, *Time-Honoured Lancaster*, 1891,
            564)

*(Geldart House* later *Queen's Head)* (see *Queen's Head*) Church Street

## George Market Street

This ancient inn on the north side of Market Street almost certainly goes back beyond the seventeenth century and was in its day the premier inn of Lancaster. In 1634 it was kept by Edmund Covell (brother of Thomas Covell, gaoler at the Castle) and a group of three officers from the Norwich garrison stayed here on their travels in that year (qv). It stood 'over against' (opposite) the *King's Arms*. Documents relating to this and other property in 1690 survive (Library MS 4483). By 1722 it was just a tenement 'formerly called the George Inn'.

| | |
|---|---|
| –1634 | Edmund Covell, brother of Thomas Covell gaoler at Castle (E. Kennerley, 'Lancaster Inns & Alehouses 1600–1730', *Lancashire Local Historian*, 5, 1990, 42; will (LRO, WRW/A 1634) |
| 1659–85 | William Waller (E. Kennerley, 'Lancaster Inns & Alehouses 1600–1730', *Lancashire Local Historian*, 5, 1990, 42) |
| 1722 | Deeds in Library (Library MS 4485) refer to tenement 'formerly called the George Inn' |

## George St Nicholas Street

| | |
|---|---|
| 1735 | House called 'the George' referred to in will of Robert Lawson (LRO WRW/A, 1736) |

## George (III) St Leonardgate

| | |
|---|---|
| 1794 | John Austin |
| 1803 | Joseph 'Sergeant' Redmayne |
| 1805 | Advert to let 'Part of George Inn, as public or private house. Enquiries to Mr Gillow'. (*Lancaster Gazette*, 18/5/1805) |
| 1805 | William Backhouse |

## George The Third (see *King's Head*) Chapel Street

## George & Dragon — Church Street

1779        George Robinson (Stallenge Rolls)

## George & Dragon — Market Street

(W. King suggests this became *Queen's*)
One of the ancient inns in Market Square, along with the *Royal Oak* and *Blue Anchor*; the *Commercial Inn* appeared later. It is first recorded in 1766 when it had 17 windows taxed (Kennerley, MS 8783), and is last named in 1856. The frontage may be seen in a watercolour drawing of the Market Square in *c*.1770 in the Whitworth Gallery, Manchester. It may have been renamed *Queen's Hotel* in 1864. The evidence from the corrupt 1865 Election indicates that either the two were the same, or else interconnected. In any case this is noted by Richard Bond as one of those inns closed within his lifetime (1820–91).

| | |
|---|---|
| 1766 | had 17 windows taxed (Kennerley, MS 8783) |
| 1766–99 | James Bland |
| 1818–22 | Ann Sergeant |
| 1825–34 | Matthew Gardner |
| 1844–51 | Jane Gardner |
| –1854 | James Gardner |
| 1854 | Myles Brockbank |
| –1855 | Robert Tate |
| 1855 | Margaret Tate |
| 1855 | William Gardner |
| 1856 | Eliza Horrocks |

## George & Dragon (formerly *St George's Tavern*) — 24 St George's Quay

This inn stands upon St George's Quay, between Elm Street and Duke Street. It is first mentioned in 1818. In 1851 it was renamed *George & Dragon*.

| | |
|---|---|
| 1818 | John Brown |
| 1822 | James Hawthornthwaite |
| 1825–28 | John Singleton |
| 1834 | Stephen Vennall |
| 1844–51 | Dorothy Hill |
| 1851 | renamed as *George & Dragon* |
| 1856 | Thomas Crampton |
| 1865 | Robert Curwen (Election Petition) |
| 1871–72 | Thomas Smith |
| 1881 | (Census) Thomas Paterson |
| 1886 | David J. N Patterson |
| 1889–90 | J. Clayton |
| 1896 | R. Miller |
| 1901 | H. Firmin |

| | |
|---|---|
| 1906 | Chief Constable objected to renewal of license, but apparently still granted (*Lancaster Guardian*, 3/3/1906) |
| 1913 | A. Wells |
| 1929 | ? |
| 1934 | F. W. Beacham |
| 1956–57 | ? |
| 1970 | D. S. Doey |
| 2006 | Punch Taverns plc (now Admiral Taverns) |

*George & Dragon*, St George's Quay.

## Golden Anchor                                                      St Nicholas Street

| | |
|---|---|
| 1753–58 | (E. Kennerley; Library MS 8783) |
| 1753 | Port Commission meets at Mrs Jennet Whiteside, at the sign of the *Golden Anchor* |

**Golden Ball** Market Street

Lying on the south side of Market Street, its site now marked by the HSBC Bank, this inn was established in 1758. A sale notice appeared in 1809. It is last recorded in 1864, but the yard at the side of the Bank is still named Golden Ball Yard. The inn is one noted by Richard Bond as closed within his lifetime (1820–91).

| | |
|---|---|
| 1758 | (E. Kennerley; Library MS 8783) |
| 1761 | T. 'Sergeant' Paget |
| 1779 | (E. Kennerley, 1982, 6) |
| 1789 | Mrs Paget (Library S10) |
| 1794–96 | James Bayne or Bain (Library MS 3706) |
| –1809 | Thomas Johnson. Sale of inn (*Lancaster Gazette*, 24/8/1809) |
| 1818 | James Foster |
| 1822–25 | Miles Chambers |
| 1827 | John Lythe (Recognisance in Library Scrapbook 2, pt 2, 56) |
| 1828 | Robert Booth |
| 1834 | Mary Williamson |
| 1844–54 | John Baxter, will (LRO WRW/A 1854) |
| 1855 | Ann Townson |
| 1855 | John Bibby |
| 1864–65 | Richard Burton (1865 Election Petition) |

[Noted by Richard Bond as closed within his lifetime (1820–91)]

---

**Golden Ball** 21 St Nicholas Street

This inn, which stood on the south side of St Nicholas Street, first appears in 1822. In 1965 it was demolished as part of the redevelopment of the area as the St Nicholas Arcade, which included the loss of this ancient thoroughfare.

| | |
|---|---|
| 1822 | Thomas Johnson |
| 1825 | John Parrington |
| 1828 | Peter Osbaldeson |
| 1834–35 | John Dunkley |
| 1844 | Richard Dixon. Had quoiting ground (*Leaves from Local History*) |
| 1851 | Richard Newton |
| –1854 | John McCann |
| 1854 | Robert Nightingale |
| 1855 | Joseph Dowthwaite |
| 1865–81 | Richard Townley (1865 Election Petition; 1881 Census) |
| 1886–1901 | John Nelson (1901 census) |
| 1913 | Mary Nicholson |
| 1929 | ? |
| 1934 | H. Schofield |
| 1956–57 | ? |
| 1965 | Demolished for St Nicholas Arcade |

## Golden Fleece

This old inn stood on the west side of Penny Street, near its northern end.

In 1764–78 a house on the site was converted into the inn (Cross Fleury, *Time-Honoured Lancaster*, 1891, 454). In 1825 the carrier Thomas Jennings left here every Wednesday and Saturday for Kirkby Lonsdale. A valuation of fixtures from 1876 survives in the City Museum (LM99.1). In 1890 the inn was demolished and rebuilt (Cross Fleury, *Time-Honoured Lancaster*, 1891, 454). Its successor lasted until 1934.

| | |
|---|---|
| 1764–78 | House converted into inn |
| 1810–18 | Robert Tatham. Son killed in accident in Market Square, 1810 |
| 1822 | T. Calvert |
| 1825 | untenanted |
| 1828 | Thomas Camm |
| 1834 | Robert Bainbridge |
| 1844–51 | James Wells, will (LRO WRW/A 1851) |
| 1856 | John Hodgson |
| 1864–65 | Richard Jackson (1865 Election Petition) |
| 1871–72 | John Foxcroft |
| 1876 | Valuation of fixtures etc. (LM99.1) |
| 1881 | (Census) William Curwen |
| 1886 | Thomas Southworth |
| 1889–90 | Mrs M. Southworth |
| 1890 | Inn demolished and rebuilt |
| 1896–1901 | R. Shaw |
| 1913 | J. Landsborough |
| 1929 | ? |
| 1934 | William Norman |

## Golden Fleece

| | |
|---|---|
| 1730–1825 | (E. Kennerley; Library MS 8783) |
| 1731 | no name given (Hewitson, Memoranda, I, 70) |
| 1794 | John Charnack |
| 1803 | Jonathan Coxell |
| 1818 | John Tomlinson |

## Golden Lion

33 Moor Lane

This inn on the north side of Moor Lane, at the junction with Brewery Lane, is also sometimes known as the *Whittle Springs*, after the brewery in Whittle-le-Woods which once supplied it, a prodigious feat of folk memory. Although first recorded in 1818 it has attracted spurious claims that those executed on Lancaster Moor were entitled to a last drink there, including the Lancashire Witches of 1612. In fact by the time it was built, executions were being held at the Castle, not upon the Moor. In 1865 its landlord, Anthony Allinson, was one of the leaders of the Liberal activists, providing money for drink and bribes for Liberal voters in the election, money ultimately but discreetly derived from the candidates themselves.

| | |
|---|---|
| 1818 | (?) Hamilton |
| 1820–25 | Mrs Mary Hamilton |
| 1828–34 | John Hamilton |
| 1844–51 | William Townson |
| 1855–65 | Anthony Knowles Allinson (1865 Election Petition) |
| 1871–72 | William Hayes or Hays (1881 census) |
| 1886–90 | James Thompson |
| 1896–1901 | Henry H. Postlethwaite (1901 census) |
| 1913 | W. C. Smith |
| 1929 | ? |
| 1934 | Albert Heavyside |
| 1956–57 | ? |
| 1970 | A. Hodgson |
| 2003 | D. O'Hara |
| 2006 | Trust Inns Ltd. |

*Golden Lion*, Moor Lane.

**Golden Shovel** (see *Malt Shovel*)                    Penny Street/Spring Garden Street

1790         Masons met there (Hewitson, Memoranda, I, 10)


**(Golden) Talbot**                                                      China Street

1766         (?) Wilson (Rule Book 1736–84, ff37–8) (Inn sign mentioned)
1828         Robert Taylor


**Grapes**                                                              Church Street

1793         Masons met there (Hewitson, Memoranda, I, 10)
1794         William Hargraves
1801–3       John Kelsey (Library S10)
1802         4 August dinner held here


**Grasshopper**                                                         Cheapside

Pre 1900     Ceased as inn (J. R. Spalding, Notes in Library)


**Gray (Grey) Horse**                                    Damside Street/Rosemary Lane

1820–44      J. Breaks
[Noted by Richard Bond as closed within his lifetime (1820–91)]


**Gray (Grey) Horse**                                                   Cable Street

Opened after closure of inn of same name on Damside Street? (J. R. Spalding, Notes in
Library)
1962         Demolished


**Greaves Hotel**                                                       Greaves Road

(license transferred from *Lord Nelson* and *Spink Bull*, China Street)
1900         (LRO deposited plans no 1893)
1902         Built
1913         G. Pearson
1929         ?
1934         Elizabeth Pearson
1956–57      ?
1970         I. H. Wilkinson
2006         Mitchell's of Lancaster (Brewers) Ltd.

### Green Ayre (Wetherspoons)  North Road

Recent
| | |
|---|---|
| 2006 | J. D. Wetherspoon plc |

---

### Green Dragon  Pudding Lane/Cheapside

This old inn stood on the east side of Cheapside, then called Pudding Lane. It is first recorded in 1772. The Rule Book gives a detailed description of the inn in 1806 (Rule Book 1784–1822, f.88). In 1848 Mr Preston, the landlord, was fined for smuggling whisky into the Castle (Cross-Fleury, *Time-Honoured Lancaster*, 1891, 580). It last appears in 1864.

| | |
|---|---|
| 1772–90 | James Bland (Egerton MS, John Rylands Library; will (LRO, WRW/A 1790) |
| 1794 | John Fawcet |
| 1803–6 | John Jackson |
| 1815–20 | Thomas 'Sergeant' Camm (Library Scrapbook 6, pt 1, 10) |
| 1820–22 | J. Porter (Library Scrapbook 6, pt 2, 29) |
| 1825 | Anthony Winder |
| 1828 | William Birkett |
| 1834 | John Hartley |
| 1844–48 | John Preston |
| 1851 | Thomas Alston |
| –1854 | Thomas Jackson |
| 1854 | Thomas Smith |
| 1864 | John Myers |

[Noted by Richard Bond as closed within his lifetime (1820–91)]

---

### Green Hare (Could this be *Green Ayre?*)  ?

| | |
|---|---|
| 1772 | Robert Bannister (Egerton MS, John Rylands Library) |

---

### Green Man  ?

| | |
|---|---|
| 1772 | Richard Walton (Egerton MS, John Rylands Library) |

---

### Hand & Heart (or *Hand on Heart*)  Skerton

| | |
|---|---|
| 1854 | Advertised to be let |
| ? | Thomas Winder (Cross Fleury, *Time-Honoured Lancaster*, 1891, 564) |
| 1865 | Mrs Winder (Election petition) |

Burnt down 'long ago' (1906)

## Hatters' Arms                                                                 Bridge Lane

1852–66     (E. Kennerley; Library MS 8783)
1820–74     Thomas Abbot (W. King in Lancaster Inns & Public Houses folder)
1865        Richard Baines (Election petition)
[Noted by Richard Bond as closed within his lifetime (1820–91)]


## Highland Laddie                                                               Penny Street

1859        *Lancaster Guardian, 23/7/1859*
[Noted by Richard Bond as closed within his lifetime (1820–91)]


## Hole in the Wall                                                              3 China Lane

One of the many low drinking-places in China Lane this goes back to 1781. Deeds of six houses
in China Lane used as the *Hole in the Wall* are in the LRO (LRO MBLa Deeds (Acc 4797)
Box 6). The buildings on the west side of China Lane were demolished in the 1890s for road-
widening and to remove some of the Corporation's least favourite inns and lodging houses.
The canny William Mitchell had already closed this inn in 1890 in return for a license for the
*Victoria Hotel* in West Road.

1781–1827   Deeds
1794–1803   John Ellwood
1818        Joseph Scott
1822        A. Scott
1825        John Schofield
1828        William Mathers
1834        John Pilling
1844        Thomas Woods
1851–56     William Whittingham
1871–72     Ann Gardner
1881        (Census) John McCarren
1886–90     William Greenall
(gone by 1892 OS)


## Horns Tavern (Stag Horn)                                                      China Lane

1820–70     M. Gardner (W. King in Lancaster Inns & Public Houses folder)
[Noted by Richard Bond as closed within his lifetime (1820–91)]


## Horse & Farrier                                                               Skerton

1820–74     W. Battersby (W. King in Lancaster Inns & Public Houses folder; Cross Fleury,
            *Time-Honoured Lancaster*, 1891, 564)

This ancient inn stood on the north side of Church Street, next above the *Mitre Inn*, and adjacent to the *Grapes*. Before 1707 it was kept by Henry Bracken, the father of Dr Bracken who was to distinguish himself when the Jacobite army came to Lancaster in 1745. A strange timber outbuilding in its yard acted as a theatre, and a handbill for a performance here dates from 1772. Another handbill in the Soulby Collection records the inn in 1808 under Richard Carr. In 1825 Samuel Wilson, carrier, left here for Beetham every Saturday. In 1837 it was rebuilt and ceased to act as an inn.

| | |
|---|---|
| pre 1707–1837 | (E. Kennerley; Library MS 8783) |
| 1707 | H. Bracken (Hewitson, Memoranda, II, 171) |
| 1772 | Anthony Blezard (Egerton MS, John Rylands Library) |
| 1794–1816 | Richard Carr (Library MS 3706, CRO Soulby Coll., ZS400) |
| 1816–22 | Dorothy Carr (Hewitson, Memoranda, II, 159) |
| 1825 | Robert Bainbridge |
| 1828 | Stephen Archer |
| 1828–34 | James Hurtley (Recognisance 1828 in Library Scrapbook 2, pt 2, 4) |
| 1837 | Rebuilt and ceased as inn |

[Noted by Richard Bond as closed within his lifetime (1820–91)]

Playbill for the Beggars' Opera, performed in 1772 by a travelling company in the theatre in the yard of the *Horse & Farrier Inn* in Church Street. (Lancaster Library)

The old theatre in the yard of the *Horse & Farrier Inn*, Church Street, which functioned before the theatre (now the Grand) was built in St Leonardgate in 1782. (Courtesy of Lancaster City Museum part of Lancashire Museums)

### *Horse & Farrier* (Beerhouse)  16 Brock Street

This inn stands on the south side of Brock Street. It is first recorded as a beerhouse in 1863. It was sold in 1923.

| | |
|---|---|
| 1863 | (K. Greenhalgh's notes in Library) |
| 1865 | James Crook (Election Petition) |
| 1881 | (Census) Elizabeth Hopkins |
| 1886 | Alexander Kerr |
| 1889–90 | J. A. Murray |
| 1896 | H. Firmin |
| 1901 | R. Winder |
| 1913 | J. Wright |
| 1923 | Sale catalogue (Library S1/62) |
| 1929 | ? |
| 1934 | Alexander Walker |
| 1956–57 | ? |
| 1970 | K. Hartley |
| 2006 | J. Lynch |
| 2008 | N. Dunne |

*Horse & Farrier*, Brock Street.

### *Hoyle's Brewery* (or *Newsham's*)  Moor Lane

1820–74   G. Hoyle (W. King in Lancaster Inns & Public Houses folder)
[Noted by Richard Bond as closed within his lifetime (1820–91)]

### *James Harford* (Beerhouse)  44 Penny Street

(Is this the same as *Brown Cow?*)

| | |
|---|---|
| 1901 | John Whittam |
| 1912 | ? (J. R. Spalding, Notes in Library) |
| 1913 | James Harford (name of licensee, rather than of pub?) |

## (Ye Olde) John O'Gaunt

55 Market Street

This inn on the south side of Market Street, between Bashful Alley and Sir Simon's Arcade, is not as old as it first appears. It is first recorded in 1871. It occupies one half of a pair of long, narrow Georgian buildings, its site constrained by the size and shape of medieval burgage plots in this part of the town. At the time of writing this is one of the most traditional inns in the city centre and recently one with a very loyal clientele, especially for jazz sessions.

| 1871–72 | Jane Forrest |
| 1881 | (Census) James Newsham |
| 1886–90 | Robert Harling |
| 1896–1901 | Jane Harling |
| 1913 | J. M. Edington |
| 1929 | ? |
| 1934 | William King |
| 1956–57 | ? |
| 1970 | A. T. Barnes |
| 1986–2004 | Steven Thorne |
| 2004 | Robin Edmundson |
| 2006 | R. Edmundson |

*(Ye Olde) John O'Gaunt*, Market Street.

## John of Gaunt

St Leonardgate

1804–45    (E. Kennerley; Library MS 8783)

## John O'Gaunt

Torrisholme Road, Skerton

Recent    (J. R. Spalding, Notes in Library)

## Kelsall's Vaults (see *Stonemasons' Arms*)

48–50 Penny Street

(succeeded by *King Edward?*)
1892    Shown on large scale OS
1901    W. Blackwell

*Keystones Scream* (now the *Pendle Witch*)            Penny Street

2006
2008         renamed the *Pendle Witch*

---

## *(Royal) King's Arms*            75 Market Street

Although the present buildings are plainly high Victorian in style this hotel on the south side of Market Street, at the junction with King Street, occupies a very old site. Before 1879 its appearance suggested that it had expanded through a number of neighbouring eighteenth-century buildings, and their frontages have rather determined the odd 'footprint' of the site today.

Its origins are obscure. Perhaps its first landlord was James Hardman, who lost all in the Royalist siege of Lancaster in 1643. John Hunter was the innkeeper in 1664 and he paid duty on 10 hearths. By 1689 Randall Hunter was assessed on 16 hearths. At that date it had a long series of named rooms, such as 'Star Chamber', 'Halfe Moone', 'Falken' and 'Fox'. Clearly the inn was growing in size and importance.

In 1701 the inn and land were offered for sale (Hewitson, Memoranda, I, 134).

*Left*: The pre-1879 *King's Arms Hotel*. The distinctive bow windows lighted large rooms including the large suite mentioned by Frances Sayer in 1857. Further up the street it is clear that the inn had simply extended through a number of Georgian houses, leading to the rather odd ground plan of the present building. (Lancaster City Museum)

*Right*: The rebuilt *(Royal) King's Arms Hotel* of 1879–82 as it is today, minus one of its projecting oriel windows over King Street.

A reference by Squire Blundell who lodged there in 1713 suggests that it may briefly have become the **Queen's Arms** as a compliment to Queen Anne. In 1766 it was assessed for eighty windows and by 1825, when John Pritt was the innkeeper, it had become the main coaching and posting inn, with seven named coaches calling each day. In 1818 Rev. Benjamin Newton stayed here, describing it in his diary. Charles Dickens also described it in 1857 in a short story in conjunction with Wilkie Collins. It was for centuries, after the demise of the **George**, the principal inn of Lancaster, and in many ways still is, although its fortunes rise and fall with its many changes of owner.

In the mid-nineteenth century Joseph Sly was landlord. He entertained many important guests such as Prince William of Gloucester, the Prince of Saxe Weimar, Queen Adelaide, the Queen Dowager, Prince Louis Napoleon, and, most famously of all, Charles Dickens. The latter set a short story here in 1857, published in *Household Words*, when he stayed here with Wilkie Collins ('The Lazy Tour of Two Idle Apprentices').

In 1879–82 the old building was taken down and replaced by a purpose-built structure, which survives today. A sale catalogue of 1898 is in the Library (S 1/35). The new hotel had stables which could accommodate up to 100 horses and had its own horse-bus to meet guests from the station.

| | |
|---|---|
| 1640 | James Hardman |
| 1664 | John Hunter had 10 hearths |
| 1689 | Randall Hunter, probate inventory (LRO, WRW/A 1689); 16 hearths in Kings Arms |
| 1701 | Inn and land offered for sale (Hewitson, Memoranda, I, 134) |
| 1704–5 | (*The Rake's Diary; Journal of George Hilton*, 68; '… dined … at the King's Arms …' |
| 1712 | (probate inventory) |
| 1712–13 | (Tyldesley Diary) |
| 1713–28 | Thomas Marshall. Nicholas Blundell 'lodged at Marshalls ye Signe of ye Queens Arms' (Diary) Perhaps the inn was renamed during Queen Anne's reign (E. Kennerley, *Lancaster Inns and Ale Houses 1600–1730*, 48) |
| 1732 | John Marshall (d. by 1745) (Library MS 2463) |
| 1772–81 | Joseph Reynolds (Egerton MS, John Rylands Library; Lancaster PRs) |
| 1781–95 | Thomas Coulthwaite (Stallenge Rolls) |
| 1781–1802 | J. Coulthwaite (or Cornthwaite) |
| 1796 | Thomas Coulthwaite (Library MS 3706) |
| 1802–28 | John Pritt |
| 1818 | Benjamin Newton stayed here (see Ch. 1) |
| 1829–36 | Joseph Ladyman (Inn bill; Library Scrapbook 2, pt 3, 42) |
| 1836–56 | John Pritt jnr (*Lancaster Gazette* 28/5/1836; Inn bill; Library Scrapbook 4, pt 1, 19) |
| 1856–77 | Joseph Sly |
| 1877–90 | S. Ducksbury (Cross Fleury, *Time-Honoured Lancaster*, 1891, 450) |
| 1879–82 | Rebuilt on same site |
| 1881 | William K. Stephenson |
| 1881 | (Census) James Gardner |
| 1886–90 | Samuel Ducksbury |
| 1898 | Sale catalogue (Library S 1/35) |
| 1896–1901 | J. S. Ducksbury |
| 1903 | J. Nelson Yates (Library Scrapbook 4, pt 3, 4) |
| 1913 | W. H. Blackhurst |
| 1929 | ? |
| 1934 | T. R. Blackhurst |
| 2006 | Oxford Hotel & Inns Management Ltd. |

*King Edward VII* (*The Edwardian*, then *Muse*, now *LAOne*)     48–50 Penny Street

(successor to *Kelsall's Vaults?*)
| | |
|---|---|
| 1913 | J. Whittaker |
| 1923 | Sale catalogue (Library S1/62) |
| 1929 | ? |
| 1934 | E. Johnson |
| 1956–57 | ? |
| 2003 | Renamed *Muse* |
| 2003 | I. J. Huntington |


*King's Head*     ?

| | |
|---|---|
| 1746–49 | Joseph Bainbridge (Stallenge Rolls) |


*King's Head* (see *George III*)     6 Chapel Street

| | |
|---|---|
| 1809–1887 | (E. Kennerley; Library MS 8783) |
| 1818–51 | James Hulme or Hume |
| 1856 | Robert Johnson |
| 1864–86 | Thomas Sanderson (1865 Election Petition; 1881 census) |
| 1889–90 | R. Parrington |
| 1896 | Thomas Thompson |
| 1898 | (LRO deposited plans no 1682) |


*King William*     Skerton

| | |
|---|---|
| 1820–74 | Mrs Thompson (W. King in Lancaster Inns & Public Houses folder) |


*Lancastrian* (formerly *Marton Street Vaults*, later *Lanky's*, now *The Lounge*)     Penny Street

| | |
|---|---|
| 1989–96 | Carol Jackson |
| 2003–06 | G. and C. Stringer |


*Last Orders* (see *Nag's Head*)     Church Street

| | |
|---|---|
| 2003 | C. L. Capper |
| 2006 | Honeycombe Leisure plc |


*Litten Tree*     Church Street

| | |
|---|---|
| Recent | |
| 2006 | SFI Group Ltd. |

## Lord Ashton (formerly *Station Inn*)      North Road

| 1991 | Became *Lord Ashton* |
|------|----------------------|
| 2006 | H. McMillan |

## Lord Nelson      China Lane

This inn, one of many in China Lane, stood on its west side, opposite the *Spink Bull*. It is first listed in 1822, although one might suspect with a name such as this it would be named in or around 1805, when Nelson, already a national hero, was killed at the battle of Trafalgar. In 1889–90 G. Scott was the landlord, and also owned the lodging house next door. Inns such as this, and lodging houses in general, were much disliked by the police who regarded them as hotbeds of criminality. In 1895 a planning application was made for a new building. (LRO, deposited plans, no 1477) This was presumably part of the widening and rebuilding of China Lane sponsored by the Corporation. The inn survived in its new form until 1901, and then ceased to exist. It is thought that its licence, with that of the nearby *Spink Bull*, was handed over in exchange for that at the *Greaves Hotel*.

| 1822–25 | James Foster |
|---------|--------------|
| 1828–34 | Edward Loftus or Lofthouse |
| 1844 | James Bingham |
| 1851 | Tim Longton |
| –1854 | Mrs Bindloss |
| 1854 | James Ellershaw |
| 1856 | William Binless |
| 1864 | Robert Hodgson |
| 1871–72 | Thomas H. Aunsworth |
| 1881 | (Census) John Nelson |
| 1886 | John Askew |
| 1889–90 | G. Scott (he had lodging house next door) |
| 1895 | Rebuilt |
| 1901 | George Stevens |

*Left: Lord Ashton*, North Road.

*Right:* Former *Lord Nelson Inn*, China Lane, demolished 1895 and rebuilt, but gone by 1901. (Lancaster Library)

**(Malt) Shovel** (see **Golden Shovel**)                                      Penny Street

| | |
|---|---|
| 1794 | Thomas Mackrall |
| 1803 | Christopher Prickett |
| 1818–25 | James Riley |
| 1828 | John Greenep |
| 1834 | William Atkinson |
| 1844 | William Backhouse |
| 1851 | Thomas Suart |
| –1854 | James Dowthwaite |
| 1854 | William Dowthwaite |
| 1856 | Joseph Dowthwaite |
| 1864 | John Wilcock |
| 1865 | William Jackson (Election Petition) |
| 1871–72 | William Burrow |
| 1876 | Rebuilt as shop |

[Noted by Richard Bond as closed within his lifetime (1820–91)]

---

**Mare Maid** (see **Mermaid**)                                      Church Street

---

**Marton Arms**                                      Marton Street

| | |
|---|---|
| 1820–74 | Mrs Jackson (W. King in Lancaster Inns & Public Houses folder) |
| 1851 | (E. Kennerley's notes in Library) |
| 1870 | Application for new license refused (*Lancaster Guardian*, 27/8/1870) |

[Noted by Richard Bond as closed within his lifetime (1820–91)]

---

**Marton Street Vaults** (later **Lancastrian**, then **Lanky's**, now **The Lounge**)    Marton Street

This inn in Marton Street is claimed (J. R. Spalding, Notes in Library) to have originated in 1724, but no other evidence makes it anything like as old as this. Indeed, it probably began in the late nineteenth century. It was rebuilt in the late 1960s.

| | |
|---|---|
| 1901–13 | W. J. Wilkinson |
| 1934 | Matthew Hillbeck |
| 1956–57 | ? |

---

**Masonic Tavern**                                      Market Street/China Street

| | |
|---|---|
| 1840 | To let (*Lancaster Gazette*, 2/5/1840) |

**Masons' Arms** (Beerhouse)                                            Pitt Street

to 1803     John Gosling
1851        George Lund
[Noted by Richard Bond as closed within his lifetime (1820–91)]


**Masons' Arms** (Beerhouse)                                       17 Mary Street

1855        (E. Kennerley; Library MS 8783)
1865        Benjamin Hartley (Election Petition)
1876        Sale of contents (City Museum LM99.1)
1881        Joseph Southworth
1886        Aaron Smallshaw
1889–90     F. Cornforth
1896        James Cruikshank
1901        (Census) William Watson
1906        Chief Constable objected to renewal of license (*Lancaster Guardian*, 3/3/1906)
Before 1913 Demolished


**Mechanics' Arms** (see *Dalton Arms*) (Beerhouse)          26 Parliament Street

There seem to be problems in identifying this with the *Dalton Arms* (qv) because of the overlap
in dates and differing lists of landlords.
1861        (E. Kennerley's notes in Library)
1881        (Census) William S. Ayer
1886–90     John Marshall
1913        Ellen Stevens
1929        ?
1934        John Bird
1956–57     ?
1970        P. S. Fieldhouse


**Merchants**                                                      Market Street

Recent
2006        Spirit Group Ltd.
2007        Punch Taverns plc


**Mermaid** (*Mare Maid*)                                          Church Street

This ancient inn stood at the south-west corner of Church Street and China Lane. First
recorded in 1684 it may in fact have been much older. It is one of three inns to appear by
name on the 1684 map of Lancaster redrawn by Kenneth Docton from survey sheets found at

Towneley Hall. The Probate Inventory of Robert Borranskill, gent, dating from 1726, gives a very detailed description of this inn. In 1748–49 it was sold and ceased to be an inn.

| 1684–1749 | (E. Kennerley's notes in Library) |
| 1684 | Towneley Hall Map |
| 1684 | Isa[ac] Yates |
| 1704 | (*The Rake's Diary; Journal of George Hilton*, 56; '... att the Meremaid ...' |
| 1717–26 | Robert Borranskill (Apprentice Rolls; probate inventory (LRO, WRW/A 1726) |
| 1729–31 | Margaret Borranskill (Hewitson, Memoranda, I, 70, 478) |
| 1731–35 | J. Abbott |
| 1748–49 | Sold and ceased to be an inn |

## *Midland Hotel* (later *Priory*, now *Bobbin*)      36 Cable Street

This hotel, on the south side of Cable Street, was established in 1901 and stands opposite the site of the original Green Ayre Station (Midland Railway Station), closed in the 1960s. It occupies two adjacent buildings, one probably of the 1840s and the other *c*.1901. In 1976 its name was changed to *Priory* and a major refurbishment took place in 1986. Its name was changed again in about 2001 to *Bobbin*.

| 1901 | (Census) William Williams |
| 1913 | W. Park |
| 1929 | ? |
| 1934 | Thomas Lawrenson |
| 1956–57 | ? |
| 1970 | H. Woodward |
| 1976 | J. Weiner. (Name changed to *Priory*) |
| *c*.2001 | (Name changed to *Bobbin*) |

## *Millstone*      Main Street, Skerton

This old inn stood on the west side of Main Street in Skerton, near the corner with Aldren's Lane. Its name comes from the nearby Skerton Mill, which had stood here since the Middle Ages and was demolished in the 1950s. First recorded in 1803 it was for many years associated with the Lune Fishery and the landlord in the early nineteenth century was William Carter, succeeded in 1832 by Robert Wilkinson, whose well-trained dog Jack helped him harvest vast quantities of fish by driving them into the net.

| 1803 | In existence (J. R. Spalding, Notes in Library) |
| 1815–32 | William Carter (LRO QSB3/151, QSB3/160/5/1, QSB3/168/4/1, Cross Fleury, *Time-Honoured Lancaster*, 1891, 564) |
| 1834–51 | Robert Wilkinson |
| 1856 | Robert Willan |
| 1871–72 | Gilbert Hall |
| 1881 | William Proctor |
| 1886 | James E. Heckingbottom |
| 1889–90 | N. Thornton |
| 1896–1913 | Mrs Mary Thornton |
| 1929–34 | J. Thornton |

## Mitre (Tavern)                                                      86 Church Street

This inn stood on the north side of Church Street, opposite the Judges Lodging. Its site now lies under Mitre House, a government building of 1973–75. Just above the *Mitre* stood the *Horse & Farrier* and *Grapes*. Excavations in 1974 in what must have been the back yard of the former inn revealed a pit filled with broken eighteenth-century wine bottles, pottery and vast numbers of cockle shells, presumably consumed at the *Mitre Inn*. Deeds of the property are in LCC Deeds (LCC Deeds 51/2). It is first recorded in the 1770s and by *c.*1912 had ceased to be an inn. It was demolished in 1958–59 and its site lay open as car parks between then and 1973.

| | |
|---|---|
| 1770s | (E. Kennerley; Library MS 8783) |
| 1794 | Thomas Slater |
| 1818–25 | Isaac Jackson, will (LRO WRW/A 1825) |
| 1828 | George Camm |
| 1834 | Benjamin Buckley |
| 1851 | John Kirk |
| 1856 | Elizabeth Kirk |
| 1864 | Elizabeth Row |
| 1865 | Edward Riley (Election petition) |
| 1871–72 | George James Dobson |
| 1881 | (Census) James Dobson |
| 1886–90 | Robert Veevers |
| 1895–1903 | W. Rainbird (Election Petition; Library Scrapbook 4, pt 3, 4) |
| 1913 | H. Firmin |
| *c.*1913 | (Ceased to be an inn; demolished 1958–59) |

---

## Moorlands Hotel                                                          Quarry Road

One of the new breed of 'respectable' hotels in the late Victorian suburbs, the *Moorlands* stands in Quarry Road at the corner with Dumbarton Road. It received planning permission in 1895 and the plans for building are in the LRO (LRO deposited plans no 1425). Its licence was transferred from *The Feathers* in China Lane, one of a series of inns in this area which the magistrates wished to see closed.

| | |
|---|---|
| 1895 | Built |
| 1895 | License transferred from *Feathers*, China Lane |
| 1896 | J. H. Patterson |
| 1901 | J. Brunton |
| 1913 | G. Brunton |
| 1934 | J. E. Heavyside |
| 1956–57 | ? |
| 1970 | T. E. Richardson |
| 2006 | Mitchell's of Lancaster (Brewers) Ltd. |

*Moorlands Hotel*, Quarry Road.

**Moulders' Arms** (Beerhouse)                                          Wood Street

(J.R.Spalding, Notes in Library)

1870          Application for new licence; refused (*Lancaster Guardian*, 27/8/1870)

---

**Munich's Arms**                                                       Moor Lane

1794          Molly Richardson

---

**Nag's Head** (now *Last Orders*)                              32 Church Street

The late Eija Kennerley's notes suggest that the *Nag's Head* began in Market Street in 1752 and moved to Church Street in 1768. Its early history is unclear. At all events this ancient inn, though rebuilt, occupies a site on the north side of Church Street, at the corner of Calkeld Lane, which it has held since 1768. In 1794 Scott's waggon left here every Tuesday and Friday for Manchester, returning the same days (Universal British Directory). In 1825 the following carriers left from here: John Pickthall for Cartmel every Friday and Saturday as the tides permitted, Thomas Chorley for Leeds and Halifax every Wednesday and Saturday, and Leonard Chapman for Sedbergh and Kirkby Stephen every Friday. (Baines' *Directory*). In 1898 the old inn was pulled down and rebuilt somewhat further back on a new building line. It now has a datestone on the corner 'WB 1898' with a carved horse's head (presumably the 'nag's head'). Deposited plans for the rebuilding are in the LRO (LRO deposited plans no 1643) A sale catalogue of 1923 survives in the Library (Library S1/62). In 2003 it was renamed *Last Orders*.

*Nag's Head/Last Orders*, Church Street.

| | |
|---|---|
| 1768 | (E.Kennerley; Library MS 8783) |
| 1772 | John Stevenson (Egerton MS, John Rylands Library) |
| 1793–1804 | James Pool or Poole (Stallenge Rolls; *Lancaster Gazette*, 23/8/1804) |
| 1818 | James Chew |
| 1822–29 | William Pilling (Library, billhead) |
| 1834 | Joseph Pilling |
| 1844–51 | John Calvert, will (LRO WRW/A 1851) |
| 1856 | George Danson |

| 1864 | Hugh Charnock |
| 1865 | Mrs Charnock (Election petition) |
| 1871–72 | John Rogerson |
| 1881 | (Census) John F. Clarkson |
| 1886 | Richard W. Knowles |
| 1889–90 | J. Woods |
| 1896 | R. Mashiter |
| 1898 | Pulled down and rebuilt on new building line |
| 1901 | W. G. Whalley |
| 1913 | S. Barnes |
| 1923 | Sale catalogue |
| 1929 | ? |
| 1934 | Sidney Timms |
| 1956–57 | ? |
| 1970 | R. J. Souter |
| 2003 | Renamed *Last Orders* |

## Naked Taylor                                                           Church Street

| 1683 | Lintel for John Simkin(son), 1621–84, in City Museum |
| 1684 | Marked on Towneley Hall Map |
| 1684 | William Gardner |
| 1698 | Joseph Gardner |

## New Inn                                                              Market Street

An ancient inn, despite its name, this stood up a yard on the north side of Market Street. It occupied the seventeenth-century house of John and Isabel Hodgson, which upon demolition was found to have sawn-off segments of earlier cruck-trusses forming its main roof timbers. It is first recorded in the 1760s. A detailed list of its contents, including three post-chaises, appears in the Rule Book for 1787 and in 1792 its landlord John Garth issued two handbills (CRO Soulby Coll. ZS 46, 47). A sale catalogue survives for 1795 (Library Scrapbook 2 (fol.) 268). In 1825 the carrier Thomas Uthers left here every Tuesday for Colne and Clitheroe. In 1987 it was closed and c.1990 demolished as part of the redevelopment of the old Mitchell's Brewery site, which stood directly behind it.

| 1760s | (E. Kennerley; Library MS 8783) |
| 1772 | John Capstick (Egerton MS, John Rylands Library) |
| 1784–87 | Matthew Reynolds (Stallenge Rolls; Rule Book 1784–1822, ff.9–12) |
| 1792–96 | John Garth or Garths (Sale catalogue, Library Scrapbook 2 (fol.) 268; Library Scrapbook 2, p t4, 21; Library MS 3706; LRO QSB3/132) |
| 1803–7 | Thomas Hodgson, will (LRO WRW/A Ad 1807) |
| 1818–28 | Richard Mason or Mawson |
| 1834 | Richard Moreland |
| 1844 | Agnes Carter |
| 1851 | John Shepherd |
| 1856 | John Bradley |
| 1864–65 | John Parkinson (Election petition) |

| 1871–72 | Ellen Moore |
| 1881 | (Census) Sarah Thexton |
| 1886–1905 | William Smith (1895 Election petition) |
| 1913 | C. Kay |
| 1929 | ? |
| 1934 | Frank Riley |
| 1956–57 | ? |
| 1970 | J. Lindsay |
| 1987 | Closed |

Demolished *c*.1990

---

### Old Sir Simon's                                                      Market Street

This ancient inn stood on the south side of Market Street immediately to the right of Sir Simon's Arcade, which is named after it. Although the late Eija Kennerley's notes in the Library suggest a date as early as 1714, this seems unlikely, as the inn was named after Sir Simon Lovat, executed after the 1745 Jacobite Rebellion. Sir Simon's portrait, by Hogarth, was very well-known, and probably formed the basis of the inn sign. (S. Shesgreen (ed.), Engravings by Hogarth, 1973, 58) The inn is first mentioned in 1757, when Thomas Crozer, innholder, appears in the Militia Ballot List. His widow was still there in 1772. In 1794 a waggon left here every Monday and Thursday for the Castle Inn, Wood Street, London, returning Tuesday and Friday (Universal British Directory). In 1825 the following carriers left from here; John Rigg for Cartmel, Ulverston and Hawkshead every Tuesday and Friday as the tides permitted, J. Sampson for Kendal and Milnthorpe every Saturday, Thomas Clarkson for Pilling every Saturday, and James Bell for Poulton le Fylde every Friday. (Baines' Directory) An inn bill of Henry Calvert survives from 1837 (Library Scrapbook 4, pt 1). In the latter days of coaching it became one of the principal coaching inns. In December 1846, when he arrived to take up his curacy at Claughton, Canon Grenside later recalled, there were still long signboards outside the *Old Sir Simon's*, showing the destinations of many of the coaches. In 1865 the inn became a shop, and it is among those noted by Richard Bond as closed within his lifetime (1820–91).

| 1714 | (E. Kennerley; Library MS 8783) |
| 1757 | Thomas Crozer (Militia Ballot List) |
| 1772 | Margaret Crozer (Egerton MS, John Rylands Library) |
| 1794 | James Wilson |
| 1803 | ? |
| 1811 | Gawen Heaton |
| 1818–23 | Henry King, will (LRO WRW/A 1823) |
| 1825–29 | Henry Calvert (Inn bill; Library Scrapbook 2, pt 3, 42) |
| 1834–36 | John Holme, will (LRO WRW/A 1836) |
| 1837 | Henry Calvert (Inn bill; Library Scrapbook 4, pt 1) |
| –1843 | E. Lofthouse |
| 1843–47 | William Bagot (*Lancaster Gazette*, 27/5/1843; Library S10) |
| 1851–56 | Edward Lofthouse, will (LRO WRW/A 1856) |
| 1864–65 | Elizabeth Lofthouse (1865 Election Petition) |
| 1865 | Became shop |

## Old Brewery Yard/Brewery Hotel Edward Street

1820–74      W. Walker (W. King in Lancaster Inns & Public Houses folder)

## Packet Boat ?

(Probably another name for *White Cross*, qv)
1865         (Election Petition)

## Paddy Mulligan's (formerly *White Horse*, now *Stonewell Tavern*) Church Street

2003         D. Cashin

## Painters' Arms Pitt Street

1820         J. Leeming (W. King in Lancaster Inns & Public Houses folder)

## Park Hotel St Oswald Street

This hotel, one of the late Victorian 'respectable' suburban houses, stands on the north side of St Oswald Street, on the corner of Prospect Street. It was founded in 1890 when Yates & Jackson, the brewers, transferred the license from the *Volunteer Inn*, in China Lane, after a struggle with the magistrates. Presumably it was intended to serve the Primrose estate, although the army was also concerned that young soldiers in the nearby Barracks might be led astray.

| | |
|---|---|
| 1890 | Yates & Jackson transferred license from *Volunteer Inn*, China Lane |
| 1896–1913 | William Brown |
| 1929 | ? |
| 1934 | Alice M. Newsham |
| 1956–57 | ? |
| 1970 | E. J. Donaldson |
| 2006 | I. and J. A. Rawcliffe |

## Penny Bank (in former premises of the Yorkshire (Penny) Bank, hence the name) Penny Street

2003         G. Carney
2006         T. J. Tomlinson

*Penny Street Bridge* (see *Farmers' Arms*)                              Penny Street

2006          A. R. Williams

*White Cross/Farmers' Arms/*
*Penny Street Bridge*, Penny Street.

---

*Phoenix Inn*                                                    Parliament Street

(See *Dalton Arms* and *Mechanics' Arms*. Said to be identifiable with these, but seems unlikely)
1820–74     G. Thomas (W. King in Lancaster Inns & Public Houses folder)
1855        Advertised to be let

---

*Pilot Boat Inn* (Beerhouse)                                          Bridge Lane

(Had date stone Y/IE 1687 over door, probably from period as private house but may have been inn even then)
1773        (E. Kennerley; Library MS 8783)
1790–96     James Dawson (Stallenge Rolls; Library MS 3706)
1835        Robinson Cumpsty (injured while firing salute for King's birthday)
1820–74     Lawson Swain (source W. King in Lancaster Inns & Public Houses folder)
1851        Lawson Swann
[Noted by Richard Bond as closed within his lifetime (1820–91)]
1939        (Building demolished as part of re-routing of Bridge Lane)

*Plasterers' Arms (Plaisterers' Arms)* Wood Street

This old inn which stood in Wood Street is first recorded in 1757 when its landlord Thomas Spence appears in the Militia Ballot List. He was still there in 1772. It is last listed in 1886 and is among those noted by Richard Bond as closed within his lifetime (1820–91). However, it is rather curiously noted as an off-licence in 1934. Whether this was a brief reincarnation or whether it had lingered on unrecorded in this role is unknown.

| | |
|---|---|
| 1757–72 | Thomas Spence (Militia Ballot List; Egerton MS, John Rylands Library) |
| 1790–96 | John Dobson (Stallenge Rolls; Library MS 3706) |
| 1818–22 | J. Woodhouse |
| 1825–28 | Thomas Brackin |
| 1834 | Edward Johnson |
| 1844 | James Atkinson |
| 1851 | James Haythornthwaite, will (LRO WRW/A 1851) |
| 1855 | Jane Hawthornthwaite |
| 1865 | Mrs Wright (married name of above; Election Petition) |
| 1886 | William Webster |

[Noted by Richard Bond as closed within his lifetime (1820–91) but recorded as off-licence in 1934 H. Jackson]

---

*Plough* 2 Bryer Street/Moor Lane

This inn stood on the south side of Moor Lane, on the corner of Bryer Street. Its deeds are in LCC Deeds (LCC Deeds 192/4A). It first appeared in 1818 and ran through to 1985 when it was for sale, in bad condition. It subsequently ceased to be an inn, and for a while was a women's refuge before being redeveloped for housing.

| | |
|---|---|
| 1818–28 | Jane Clemison or Cleminson |
| 1834 | George Cleminson |
| 1844 | James T? |
| 1851 | Thomas Hall |
| –1854 | Robert Nightingale |
| 1854 | Isabella Moore |
| 1855 | George Cowperthwaite |
| ? | William Speight |
| 1857 | Robert Nightingale |
| 1864–65 | John Wearden (Election Petition) |
| 1871–72 | Henry Pilkington |
| 1881 | Matthew Goth |
| 1886–90 | Harvey Pinchon |
| 1896 | J. Brunton |
| 1901–13 | Richard Loxam (1901 Census) |
| 1929 | ? |
| 1934 | John Garth |
| 1956–57 | ? |
| 1970 | R. Edwards |
| 1985 | For sale, in bad condition. Subsequently ceased as inn. |

**Prince Albert** (Beerhouse)                                                    Chapel Street

[Noted by Richard Bond as closed within his lifetime (1820–91)]

---

**Prince Of Wales** (see *Feathers*)                                             Market Street

---

**Prince William** (Beerhouse)                                        28 George Street

| | |
|---|---|
| 1820–74 | Mrs Smith (W. King in Lancaster Inns & Public Houses folder) |
| 1865 | Robert Smith (Election Petition) |
| 1870 | Application for new licence (*Lancaster Guardian*, 27/8/1870) |
| 1881 | (Census) Nancy Smith |
| 1886–90 | James M. Pearson |
| 1896 | F. Wolfenden |
| pre-1901 | Closed. Fanlight in Museum. Replaced by nearby *Royal Hotel* |

---

**Prince William Henry**                                          107 Penny Street

Standing at the southern end of Penny Street, just across the canal bridge, this inn was the first in Lancaster proper, for travellers from the south. With the re-routing of roads in this area in 1901 its site now lies under modern Thurnham Street. It had a large field adjacent on which cattle and horse markets and other shows were held. It first appears in 1790–92. In 1825 the carrier John Swindlehurst left here every Monday and Saturday for Dolphinholme. In 1856 it was purchased by the Corporation as a toll house, for which its position on the edge of the borough suited it. A sale catalogue for 1900 survives in the Library (Library S 1/47). In the following year it was demolished for the Penny Street Bridge improvements.

| | |
|---|---|
| 1790–92 | James Parkinson (Stallenge Rolls) |
| 1793–95 | William Leece or Leice (Stallenge Rolls) |
| 1818–26 | Francis Gardner, will (LRO WRW/A 1826) |
| 1834 | Thomas Atkinson |
| 1851 | John Sandham |
| –1855 | Edward Singleton |
| 1855 | Dorothy Nightingale |
| 1856 | purchased by Corporation as toll house (E. Kennerley; Library MS 8783) |
| 1864 | James Patterson |
| c.1865 | photograph in Museum |
| 1865–72 | John Huntington (1865 Election Petition) |
| 1881 | Henry J. W. Yates |
| 1881 | (Census) David Gill |
| 1886–90 | Charles Bond |
| 1891–95 | Mrs E. Bond |
| 1896 | E. Bond (Exors of) |
| 1899 | C. H. Bond |
| 1900 | Sale catalogue |
| c.1901 | Demolished for Penny Street Bridge improvements |

*Priory Hotel* (see *Midland,* now *Bobbin*)                                    Cable Street

*Punchbowl*                                                                St George's Quay
1794          William Noble

*Quay Carters' Arms*                                                            Skerton
1820–74      E. Nelson (W. King in Lancaster Inns & Public Houses folder)

*Queen's* (former *George & Dragon?*) (Beerhouse)                        Market Street
1864          Jacob Stanley
[Noted by Richard Bond as closed within his lifetime (1820–91)]

*Queen's Head*                                                              Church Street

This ancient inn stood on the north side of Church Street, where the Masonic Hall now stands.
The present Masonic Hall, although refronted in the 1880s, still maintains its seventeenth-
century back and staircase, which must have belonged to the inn. It is first recorded in 1772,
although noted elsewhere as formerly a private house of Charles Lambert, fitted up for John
Carr in 1804. John Carr issued a handbill in 1806, now in the Library. In 1825 the carrier Miles
Sorer left here every Tuesday and Saturday for Milnthorpe. In 1884 the site was purchased
by the various lodges of Masons for their first Masonic Hall (Cross-Fleury, *Time-Honoured
Lancaster,* 473). Previously they had met in various inns. The **Queen's Head** is one of those noted
by Richard Bond as closed within his lifetime (1820–91).

| | |
|---|---|
| 1772 | Richard Crosfield (Egerton MS, John Rylands Library) |
| 1775–77 | (?) Whiteside (late *Geldart House,* Stallenge Rolls) |
| 1796 | John Austen (Library MS 3706) |
| 1804 | Noted as formerly a private house of Charles Lambert, fitted up for John Carr (J. R. Spalding, Notes in Library) |
| 1803–17 | John Carr (Library broadsheet; *Lancaster Gazette* 24/8/1809; Library Scrapbook 6, pt 1, 21v; will (LRO WRW/A 1817) |
| 1818–22 | William Newton |
| 1822 | For sale |
| 1825–28 | John Mattinson |
| 1834 | Elizabeth Tatham |
| 1844 | Thomas Dixon |
| 1851 | Mary Wilson |
| 1856 | Mary Maychell |
| 1864 | Hannah Murphy |
| 1865 | Michael Murphy (Election petition) |
| 1884 | Site purchased by Masons for Masonic Hall |

[Noted by Richard Bond as closed within his lifetime (1820–91)]

### Queen's Hotel (former *White Lion*)    3 Penny Street

1871–72     William B. Baxter
1881        George Bargh
1886–96     William J. Lamb
1901        R. Bennett
1903        Frederick Price (Library
            Scrapbook 4, pt 3, 4)
1913        E. Johnson
1929        F. G. Ferris
1934        Robert Fothergill
1936–37     Demolished to make way
            for Woolworths

Former *Queen's Hotel*, Penny Street.
(Lancaster Library)

---

### Railton Hotel    Station Road

1970        N. A. Falconer

---

### Railway Inn (? predecessor to *Albert Inn*)    King Street (note Railway Inn Yard)

1839        To let, Mr Saul owner (*Lancaster Guardian*, 3/8/1839)
1844        Thomas Atkinson
[Noted by Richard Bond as closed within his lifetime (1820–91)]

---

### Rainbow    New Street

1751–72     (E. Kennerley; Library MS 8783)
1751–57     Richard Fayrer (Militia Ballot List)
1772        W. Barnes' creditors' meeting held here

---

### Ram's Head (is this the same as *Bull's Head*?)    Cheapside

Late seventeenth century (Kennerley 1982, 5)
1687        (J. R. Spalding, Notes in Library)
1764        (?) Barlow (Rule Book 1736–84, ff29–31; inn sign listed)

## Red Cross
*Spring Garden Street*

| | |
|---|---|
| 1758–1864 | Deeds relating to site of former *Red Cross* (LRO MBLa Deeds (Acc 4797) Box 4) |
| 1794 | George Taylor |
| 1820–74 | Henry Leach (W. King in Inns & Public Houses folder) |

## Red Cross
*Market Street*

| | |
|---|---|
| 1818 | Mary Chadwick |
| 1821 | (E. Kennerley; Library MS 8783) |

## Red Cross
*1 Owen Road, Skerton*

This inn stood on the west side of Owen Road, near Skerton Bridge.

It is first mentioned in 1815, when a public meeting was held here, while the landlord, Thomas Clough, appears in the same year in the alehouse recognisances (LRO, QSB3/151). It is possible, though that the 'Red Lion at the Bridge Foot' was a misnaming of this inn in 1745 (see *Red Lion*), which would make it much older. However, Skerton Bridge was not yet built at this date and the mystery remains. When Skerton underwent major rebuilding in 1959–62 the inn was rebuilt on new site among a parade of shops about 50 metres further back, in a brutal concrete style. By 2003 it was closed and derelict, and in 2004 it was demolished and the site reused.

| | |
|---|---|
| 1815 | Public meeting held there |
| 1815–23 | Thomas Clough (LRO QSB3/151; will (LRO WRW/A 1823) |
| 1823 | Jane Clough (LRO QSB3/160/5/1) |
| 1825–34 | Thomas Wilson (LRO QSB3/168/4/1) |
| 1839 | To let, in possession of Mrs Wilson (*Lancaster Guardian*, 19/10/1839) |
| 1844 | William Atkinson |
| 1851 | Gilbert Hall |
| 1856 | Mary Ann and Margaret Slinger |
| 1865 | William Barrow (Election Petition) |
| 1871–72 | Robert B. Ellershaw |
| 1881 | Margaret Kirkby |
| 1886–90 | Christopher Gardner |
| 1896–1913 | T. M. Cairns |
| 1929 | ? |
| 1934 | Margaret Cairns |
| 1956–57 | ? |
| 1962 | Rebuilt on new site about 50m to rear |
| 1970 | G. Howarth |
| 2003 | Closed and derelict |
| 2004 | Demolished and site reused |

## Red Flag
*Rosemary Lane*

| | |
|---|---|
| 1854 | James Townley (*Lancaster Guardian* 16/9/1854) |

[Noted by Richard Bond as closed within his lifetime (1820–91)]

*Red Lion*                                                               21 Church Street

Standing on the south side of Lower Church Street, next to the corner of Cheapside, this
ancient inn was recorded before 1711 when Judith Hunter held it on lease from the Corporation.
A drawing in the Binns Collection at Liverpool shows the inn in the early nineteenth century
as a long, low building with mullioned windows. A sale notice for the inn appears in the
*Lancaster Gazette*, 23/8/1804. Deeds of various properties including the *Red Lion* with yard are
in the LRO (MBLa Deeds (Acc 4797) Box 21). It is last listed in 1913.

| | |
|---|---|
| pre 1711 | Judith Hunter (E. Kennerley; Library MS 8783) |
| 1794 | Thomas Bland |
| 1804 | Robert Lightburn (sale of inn, *Lancaster Gazette*, 23/8/1804) |
| 1818–22 | John Holden |
| 1825–34 | James Wells or Willis |
| 1837–92 | Deeds of various property inc. Red Lion with yard (LRO MBLa Deeds (Acc 4797) Box 21) |
| 1844 | George Bloom |
| 1851 | James Kitchen |
| 1856? | Jane Kitchen |
| –1855 | Edward Colman |
| 1855 | John Ball |
| 1864 | John Ball |
| 1865–72 | John Batty (1865 Election petition) |
| 1881 | (Census) William Ball |
| 1886–90 | John Wilson |
| 1895–96 | J. W. Batty (1895 Election petition) |
| *c*.1900 | E. Wilson (photo) |
| 1901 | Mrs E. Wilson |
| 1913 | P. H. Heyes |

*Red Lion*                                                         Bridge Lane or Skerton?

| | |
|---|---|
| 1745 | The landlord of the *Red Lion* at the Bridge Foot rented out rooms to those who wished to see Bonnie Prince Charlie come in (see also *Red Cross*, Skerton) |

*Reds Café Bar* (now renamed *Mint Café Bar*)                              Church Street

Recent

| | |
|---|---|
| 2006 | C. Horn |

*Refreshment Rooms*                                                       Castle Station

| | |
|---|---|
| 1820–74 | Mrs Prikett (W. King in Inns & Public Houses folder) |
| 1886 | A. Rose |

**Richard Gillow**                                                    Market Street

Recent


**Ridge Hotel**                                                    Patterdale Road

1962        T. and T. Stephenson


**Rileys**                                                           Church Street

Recent


**Ring of Bells** (Beerhouse)                                      St Leonardgate

1806–52     (E. Kennerley; Library MS 8783)
1806        J. Gardner
1852        T. Crook


**Ring Of Bells** (Beerhouse)                                    52–4 King Street

Originally a beerhouse this inn on the west side of King Street occupies a very fine former
private house of the early eighteenth century with a particularly splendid doorcase and hood,
carved with Roman military trophies. It
first appears in 1881, although this may
be when it gained its sign. It is not clear
which ring of bells it refers to; the peal of
eight at the Priory church or the peal of six
which used to exist at St Thomas' church
in Penny Street.

1820–74     Jane Park (W. King in Inns &
            Public Houses folder)
1881–90     Jane Park (1881 Census)
1896–1913   J. N. Taylor or Naylor
1929        ?
1934        Alice Ainsworth
1956–57     ?
1970        A. Wild
2003        Paula Cutler
2006        Mitchell's of Lancaster
            (Brewers) Ltd.

*Ring of Bells*, King Street.

## Roebuck
Penny Street

1859   (*Lancaster Guardian*, 23/7/1859)
[Noted by Richard Bond as closed within his lifetime (1820–91)]

## Rope & Anchor
Skerton

1818   E. Jackson
1828   Richard Warbreck

## Rose Tavern (Beerhouse)
52 Ullswater Road

Standing on the west side of Ullswater Road, on the corner of Dalton Road, this beerhouse is one of three licensed premises serving the Freehold estate. (See *Freeholders' Arms* and *Britannia*). It first appears in 1865, during the corrupt election of that year, when it was used for treating Liberal voters. It occupies premises little different from the terraced houses round about. By 1901 it had been acquired by Mitchells, the brewers.

| | |
|---|---|
| 1865–72 | John Long or Lang (1865 Election Petition) |
| 1881 | (Census) Joseph Taylor |
| 1886–1901 | Richard Airey |
| 1913 | E. Airey |
| 1929 | ? |
| 1934 | T. Watson |
| 1956–57 | ? |
| 1970 | M. Mawson |
| 2003 | M. J. and C. Taylor |
| 2006 | Mitchell's of Lancaster (Brewers) Ltd. |

*Rose Tavern*, Ullswater Road.

## Rose & Crown (see *Vaults* or *Tubs*)
9 Market Entrance

This inn, established in 1794, stood in the passage giving access to the Market from Market Street, and backed on to the *Slip Inn*. Although it appears on the 1892 large-scale OS map the directories do not name it between 1856 and 1913. It may have become *Dale's Vaults* at this period, named for Dale & Co., wine, spirit, ale and stout merchants. The name *Tubs* was probably unofficial, describing its prominent flower tubs. It is last recorded in 1934.

| | |
|---|---|
| 1794 | James Winray |
| 1796 | John Jackson (Library MS 3706) |
| 1817 | Henry Hogarth, will (LRO WRW/A 1817) |
| 1822–40 | William Pratt, will (LRO WRW/A 1840) |
| 1844–46 | Alice Pratt, will (LRO WRW/A 1846) |
| 1851 | Jane and Ann Pratt |
| 1856 | John Knowles |
| 1865 | Benjamin Hartley (Election petition) (Is this a mistake for *Masons' Arms?*) |

| 1889–1901 | Dale & Co; wine, spirit, ale and stout merchants |
| 1895 | (Election petition) |
| 1913 | H. Banks |
| 1934 | W. M. Wilkinson |

## *Royal Hotel* (incorporating *Latinos*) — Thurnham Street

(Replaced *Prince William* on nearby site)
This hotel, on the west side of Thurnham Street, stands next to the former Dispensary of 1833. It first appears in 1901. It belongs to a group of larger, more 'respectable' premises which the brewers saw as more likely to obtain licences at a time of caution by magistrates and of a strong Temperance movement. It probably took over from the *Prince William* beer-house just up the street, and certainly its first landlord, Mr Wolfenden, transferred from one to the other.

*Royal Hotel*, Thurnham Street.

| 1901 | F. Wolfenden |
| 1913–34 | R. E. Bamber |
| 1956–57 | ? |
| 1970 | B. Hooton |
| 2003–5 | Dawn Pearson |
| 2005 | Part renamed *Latinos* |
| 2006 | Kirklands Entertainment Ltd. |

## *Royal Oak* — Market Street

One of the ancient inns of the Market Square, this goes back before the 1750s. In 1757 William Sharp the innkeeper appears in the Militia Ballot List and his will dated 3/12/1765 is in the LRO. His name is over the door in the watercolour drawing of Market Square in the Whitworth Art Gallery, Manchester. The inn was kept by several generations of women between 1794 and 1834; Jennet Warbrick (d.1798), Elizabeth Noon (d.1802) and Jane Noon, the last of whom issued a handbill in 1803. The inn is last listed in 1856 and is one of those noted by Richard Bond as closed within his lifetime (1820–91).

| –1750s | E. Kennerley's notes in Library |
| 1757–66 | William Sharp (Militia Ballot List; will LRO, WRW/A 1766) |
| 1772 | John Royle (Egerton MS, John Rylands Library) |
| 1794–98 | Jennet Warbrick |
| 1798–1802 | Elizabeth Noon |
| 1803–39 | Jane Noon (CRO Soulby Coll., ZS49; inn to let, *Lancaster Gazette*, 10/8/1839) |
| 1840–44 | Edward Braithwaite (Library, billheads) |
| 1851–56 | Joseph Sly (Library, billheads) |

[Noted by Richard Bond as closed within his lifetime (1820–91)]

### Royal Oak (Beerhouse)

This inn, originally a beerhouse, stands on the east side of what was once Main Street, now Mainway, in Skerton. It is one of the few of Skerton's many inns and beerhouses to survive and the only one of them not to have been rebuilt. It is first mentioned in 1881, but occupies an earlier building.

| | |
|---|---|
| 1881 | Edward Bradley |
| 1886–1913 | Thomas Cornthwaite |
| 1929 | ? |
| 1934 | T. Cornthwaite jnr |
| 1956–57 | ? |
| 2003 | W. J. Caldwell |
| 2006 | P. and G. Bowman |

*Royal Oak*, Skerton.

---

### St Georges Tavern (see *George & Dragon*)

St George's Quay

---

### Santé Restaurant & Bar

Church Street

Recent

| | |
|---|---|
| 2006 | C2 Investment Ltd |

---

### Sawyers' Arms

Damside Street

| | |
|---|---|
| 1794 | James Skirrow |
| 1818–25 | Thomas Hodgson |
| 1828 | John Thornton |
| 1834 | Margaret Speight |
| 1844 | John Atkinson |
| 1851 | Isaac Danson |
| 1853 | Jane Wadeson |
| 1855 | William Jackson |
| 1856 | George Danson |
| 1864 | James Gardner |
| 1865 | Dobson (Election petition) |
| 1871–72 | John Taylor |
| 1876 | Magistrates refused to transfer licence to *Britannia* (*Lancaster Guardian*, 30/9/1876) |
| 1880s | Demolished for Gillow's Showrooms (E. Kennerley; Library MS 8783) |

[Noted by Richard Bond as closed within his lifetime (1820–91)]

**Sawyers' Arms** (Beerhouse)     1 Rose Street

(Is this the same as *Bee Hive?*)

| | |
|---|---|
| 1864–65 | Richard Nixon (Election petition) |
| 1896 | Mrs E. Ralph |
| 1901 | (Census) Robert Ralph |

---

**Seven Stars**     King Street

| | |
|---|---|
| 1820–74 | E. Foster (W. King in Lancaster Inns & Public Houses folder) |

---

**Shakespeare (Tavern)**     96 St Leonardgate

No longer an inn, but still retaining its name as a private hotel, this stands on the north side of St Leonardgate, next to the corner of Pitt Street. It is first recorded in 1794 but may be a little earlier, given its proximity to and connection with the Theatre of 1781 (now the Grand Theatre), for which it must be named. In the early days of the University (first students 1964), which used the former premises of Waring & Gillow nearby, this was very much a university pub. In c.1985 it was closed as public house.

| | |
|---|---|
| 1794 | George Redmaynes |
| 1818–28 | Thomas Gregson |
| 1834 | Nancy Gregson |
| 1844–45 | John Brough, will (LRO WRW/A 1845) |
| 1851 | John Lodge |
| –1855 | John Wearden |
| 1855 | Miles Ellithorne |
| 1864–72 | Mary Ellen Dickenson (1865 Election petition) |
| 1881 | (Census) Elizabeth Cornthwaite |
| 1886 | John Ralph |
| 1889–96 | H. Cottam |
| 1901–34 | Herbert Swindlehurst |
| 1956–57 | ? |
| 1970 | C. Shaw |
| ? | V. Hornigold |
| c.1985 | Closed as public house |

---

**Ship** (Formerly **Cock** and **Three Squirrels** inns)     31–3 North Road

This old inn, on the south side of North Road, between Pitt Street and Mason Street, occupied the site of two older inns, the **Cock** and **Three Squirrels**, according to Cross Fleury (*Time Honoured Lancaster*, 1891, 453–4). It is listed from 1772. A succession of members of the Goth family served as landlords between 1789 and 1827. In 1789 it was the founding place for the Friendship & Union Friendly Society (Cross-Fleury, 478). In 1805 the Borough Court listed the goods of John Goth, which included two signs (the inn signs) and brewing vessels

(Rule Book 1784- 1822, f.82). A sale catalogue for 1827 is in the Library (Library S10). The inn was rebuilt in 1889, and the surviving façade with the name in relief clearly shows how it was made out of two houses. It is last listed in 1970.

| | |
|---|---|
| 1772 | Henry Whiteside (Egerton MS, John Rylands Library) |
| 1789 | Mr Goth (meeting place for Friendship & Union Friendly Society) |
| 1794 | Martha Goth |
| 1805 | John Goth |
| 1818–27 | Mrs Ellen Goth |
| 1827 | Sale catalogue |
| 1827 | Recognisance for John Moss (Library Scrapbook 2, pt 2, 1) |
| 1834–44 | John Moss, alias Evans, will (LRO WRW/A 1844) |
| 1851–56 | John Wardley |
| 1864 | William Hill |
| 1871–72 | John Wearden |
| 1881 | (Census) Samuel Dobson |
| 1886 | Robert Martindale |
| 1889 | Rebuilt |
| 1889–90 | R.Dodd (owner Mr Mitchell) |
| 1896 | R.Douglas |
| 1901 | (Census) Thomas Thompson |
| 1913 | Mary A.Thompson |
| 1929 | ? |
| 1934 | Frank Lofthouse |
| 1956–57 | ? |
| 1970 | J.Fuller |

Closed and converted into shops, but still has name on façade.

Former *Ship Inn*, North Road.

---

## *Ship* China Lane

| | |
|---|---|
| 1794 | Richard Crosfield |

---

## *Ship (Launch?)* Bridge Lane/St George's Quay

[Noted by Richard Bond as closed within his lifetime (1820–91)]

---

## *Shovel* (see *Malt Shovel*) Penny Street

## Shovel & Broom

Market Street

[Noted by Richard Bond as closed within his lifetime (1820–91)]

---

## Sir Richard Owen (Wetherspoons)

Spring Garden Street

Recent

2006    J. D. Wetherspoon plc

---

## Skerton Hotel (formerly Black Bull)

2–4 Owen Road, Skerton

| | |
|---|---|
| 1896–1901 | Mrs A. Lamb |
| 1913 | R. Lamb |
| 1917 | Sale catalogue (Library S 1/68) |
| 1929 | ? |
| 1934 | B. D. Slater |
| 1956–57 | ? |
| 1970 | W. Proctor |
| 2003 | D. Anderson |
| 2006 | Enterprise Inns plc |

---

## Slip Inn (now Fibber McGee's) (? formerly Warpers' Arms)

James Street

This old inn, perhaps originally the *Warpers' Arms*, stands on the west side of James Street, at its north end. It used to back on to the *Rose & Crown*. It appears to be first mentioned in 1776. In the mid-1990s, when the area around was redeveloped, it was renamed *Fibber McGee's*, at the height of the fashion for Irish-themed fun-pubs.

| | |
|---|---|
| 1776 | Robert Gibson (Stallenge Rolls) (? same inn?) |
| 1781 | Thomas s of Robert Gibson, Innkeeper (Lancaster PRs) |
| 1787–88 | William Preston (Stallenge Rolls) (?) |
| 1793–95 | Giles Townson |
| 1844–56 | Edward Bousfield |
| 1864–65 | Robert Lamb (1865 Election Petition) |
| 1881 | (Census) William Yates |
| 1886–90 | John Robinson |
| 1896 | John Wall |
| 1901–13 | J. Phillips |
| 1934 | John Coffey |
| 1956–57 | ? |
| 1995 | renamed *Fibber McGee's* |

*Slip Inn/Fibber McGee's*, James Street.

**Spink Bull**                                                    29 China Lane

This old inn stood on the east side of China Lane, opposite the *Lord Nelson*. The name Spink seems to mean 'spotted' in local dialect. It first appears in 1794. A sale of the inn at the *Cross Keys* in 1876 is given in a document in the City Museum (LM99.1). In 1901 the licence, with that of the *Lord Nelson*, was transferred to the *Greaves Hotel*, as part of the clearance from the new China Street of inns and beerhouses which the magistrates and Corporation thought objectionable.

| | |
|---|---|
| 1794 | Richard Kendall |
| 1818–22 | John Atkinson |
| 1825–28 | William Greenall |
| 1844 | George Askew |
| 1851 | Robert Willan |
| 1854 | Agnes Willan |
| –1855 | Joseph Dowthwaite |
| 1855 | Richard Thompson |
| 1864 | Christopher Western |
| 1865 | John Farraday (Election petition) |
| 1871–81 | William Thompson |
| 1876 | Sale of inn at Cross Keys (LM99.1) |
| 1886 | John Capstick |
| 1889–90 | C.W. Green |
| 1901 | W. Pym |

License transferred to *Greaves Hotel*

**Spinners' Arms** (Beerhouse)                                   10 Aldcliffe Lane

| | |
|---|---|
| 1820–74 | William Whitehead (W. King in Lancaster Inns & Public Houses folder) |
| 1845 | Mary Kitchen |
| 1851 | John Bramwell |
| 1865 | James Jackson (Election petition) |
| 1881 | Thomas Fairclough |
| 1881–86 | Joseph Southworth (1881 Census) |
| 1889–90 | J. Cornforth |
| 1896–1901 | Thomas Wood |
| 1906 | Chief Constable objected to renewal of license, but apparently still granted (*Lancaster Guardian* 3/3/1906) |
| 1913 | D. Richardson |
| 1934 | J.W. Burrows |
| 1956–57 | ? |

**Spread Eagle**                                           Pudding Lane/Cheapside

| | |
|---|---|
| 1794 | Richard Warbrick |
| 1818 | John Jackson |

*Station Inn* (now *Lord Ashton*) (Beerhouse)                                      36 North Road

Originally a beerhouse without a name, this stands on the north side of North Road at the junction with Nile Street. It may have begun in the mid-nineteenth century but is positively recorded from 1865 when Gardners kept it for thirty six years. Its name was changed to *Lord Ashton* in 1991.

| | |
|---|---|
| 1820–74 | R. Gardner (W. King in Inns & Public Houses folder) |
| 1865 | Edward Gardner (Election petition) |
| 1881–1901 | Ellen Gardner (1881 Census) |
| 1913 | Mary Standen |
| 1929 | ? |
| 1934 | John Lancaster |
| 1956–57 | ? |
| 1970 | H. Stephenson |
| 1991 | Became *Lord Ashton* |

*Stonemasons' Arms* (then *Kelsall's Vaults*, then *King Edward VII*,
then *The Edwardian*, then *Muse*, now *LAOne*)                          50–2 Penny Street

The succession of names on this site is far from proven, but seems plausible. The inn lies on the west side of Penny Street, between Common Garden and Spring Garden Streets. From 1794 to 1844 it was the *Stonemasons' Arms*, and between 1892 and 1901 *Kelsall's Vaults*. Then from 1913 to the 1970s it was the *King Edward VII*, and from 1970s to 2003 *The Edwardian*. In 2003 it had a short-lived change of name to *Muse* and in 2004 became *LAOne*. The frontage appeared to be Edwardian, but was rebuilt in 2005 in a bland style. There is a sale catalogue of 1923 in the Library (Library S1/62).

| | |
|---|---|
| 1794 | William Lee |
| 1818 | J. Croudson |
| 1822 | Thomas Croudson |
| 1825 | Mary Croudson |
| 1828–34 | Nancy Croudson |
| 1844 | Bryan Edmondson |

*Stonewell Tavern* (formerly *White Horse*, then *Paddy Mulligan's*,
now once again *Stonewell Tavern*)                                       Church Street

| | |
|---|---|
| 2006 | C. Webber |

This ancient inn on the south side of Church Street, at the corner of Sun Street, goes back to at least the 1680s, making it one of Lancaster's oldest inns in continuous existence. It appears obliquely on the 1684 plan of Lancaster redrawn by Kenneth Docton from survey sheets found at Towneley Hall as 'Sun Stables'. The stables were separated from the main inn, which stood within a large courtyard building called Stoop Hall, perhaps late medieval in origin, and belonging to the Molyneux family, Earls of Sefton. In 1705 Joseph Taylor stayed here on his way to Edinburgh. In 1745 Lords Murray and Elcho stayed here on their march south with the Jacobite forces. The Militia Ballot List of 1757 lists the landlord, Thomas Beck, along with George Atkinson, Jno Bowstead, Robert Hamilton, Samuel Winder and Henry Bleasdale, all servants at the *Sun Inn*. It had a good bowling green in 1767, according to an advert (Hewitson Memoranda, I, 181). In 1783 the tenant, Stanley Turner gave notice, citing the poor condition of building (E. Kennerley; Library MS 8783), and in 1785 the inn was rebuilt as part of the redevelopment by the Carter brothers, who had acquired the land from the Molyneux family. This is essentially the inn that survives today. In 1825 Mary Clark, carrier, left here for Beetham every Saturday. The inn was extensively refurbished in 2003 and in 2006 was extended into the neighbouring house, 65 Church Street.

| | |
|---|---|
| 1680s- | (E. Kennerley; Library MS 8783) |
| 1700 | George Foxcroft (Hewitson, Memoranda, I, 136) |
| 1706 | Burial of son of George Foxcroft, innkeeper (Lancaster PRs) |
| 1705 | Joseph Taylor stayed here on way to Edinburgh (Cowan ed., 1903, 161) |
| 1711–12 | George Foxcroft took lease of 3 lives from Lord Molyneux (LRO DDM/53/8) |
| 1712–13 | (Tyldesley Diary) |
| 1722–23 | *The Rake's Diary; Journal of George Hilton*, 71; '... went to the Sun ...' |
| 1745 | (Hewitson, Memoranda, I, 365) |
| 1728 | Jane Rawlinson innkeeper (Hewitson, Memoranda, I, 70) |
| 1735–69 | Isaac Rawlinson innkeeper (Hewitson, Memoranda, 166, 90; will LRO, WRW/A 1769) |
| 1757–68 | Thomas Beck (Militia Ballot List; will LRO, WRW/A 1768) |
| 1772–75 | Joseph Norman (Egerton MS, John Rylands Library; christening of d. of Joseph Norman, innkeeper (Lancaster PRs) |
| 1777 | Belonged to Elizabeth Brown |
| 1777–83 | Stanley Turner (E. Kennerley; Library MS 8783) |
| 1784 | Henry Addison |

Internal partition of wattle and daub found when the *Sun Inn* was refurbished in 2003.

A rather fanciful reconstruction by Fred Kirk Shaw for the Lancaster Pageant in 1913 of Bonnie Prince Charlie arriving in Lancaster. He is pictured outside 76 Church Street, although he probably did not in fact stay there, but further up the street. Many inns are mentioned in the accounts of the Jacobites' arrival in 1745, including the *Sun Inn* opposite, where several of the leaders of the army were billeted. Inns were chosen because they could accommodate men and horses in comfort and had stocks of food and drink already.
(Courtesy of Lancaster City Museum part of Lancashire Museums)

| | |
|---|---|
| 1785 | Inn rebuilt |
| 1786 | James Parkinson |
| 1793–94 | Thomas Bouskill (Stallenge Rolls) |
| 1795–96 | Elizabeth Bouskill or Bowskill (Stallenge Rolls; Library MS 3706) |
| 1798–1802 | Thomas White d. (will LRO WRW/A 1802) |
| 1803 | John Rimmer (Rule Book 1784–1822, ff.64–6; bankrupt *Lancaster Gazette*, 28/5/1803) |
| 1803 | William Hartley |
| 1816–25 | John Bagot (Library Scrapbook 6, pt 1, 22) |
| 1828–43 | William Bagot |
| 1843–44 | Edward Lofthouse (*Lancaster Gazette* 3/6/1843) |
| 1851 | Benjamin Hartley |
| 1864–72 | John Bannister (1865 Election petition) |
| 1881 | (Census) Winn Scott |
| 1886–96 | Benjamin Howson |
| 1901 | G. W. Howson |
| 1913 | Rose E. Howson |
| 1926 | Yates & Jackson |
| 1929 | ? |
| 1934 | E. M. Townson |
| 1956–57 | ? |
| 1970 | J. B. Holding |
| 1984 | R & L Kiziuk |
| 2003 | Refurbished |
| 2006 | C2 Investment Ltd. |
| 2006 | Extended |

The *Sun Inn*, from Mackreth's map of Lancaster in 1778. The inn then occupied part of a large building around a courtyard called Stoop or Stewp Hall, owned by the Sefton family. It may have been of medieval or 17th century date, and was named after the *stoops* or columns which it presented to Church Street.

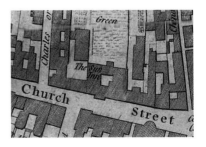

*Swan With Two Necks* (see *White Swan*) St Nicholas Street

---

*Swan With Two Necks* (hence Swan Court) Stonewell/St Leonardgate

1698/9      (E. Kennerley; Library MS 8783)
1701–29      Thomas Gibson (datestone in Swan Court G/TI 1701; Tyldesley Diary; LCC Deeds 198/2:13)

---

*Swan With Two Necks* Bridge Lane

1790      John Jackson (Stallenge Rolls)
1796      John Ashburner (Library MS 3706)

---

*Talbot* Market Street

1730–56      (E. Kennerley; Library MS 8783)
–1752      Thomas Birchall, will (LRO, WRW/A 1752)
1756      Elizabeth Birchall

---

*Thistle & Crown* (see *White Hart*) Church Street/North Road

1732–82      (E. Kennerley; Library MS 8783)
1732–47      William Spence (Hewitson, Memoranda, I, 70, 132)
–1782      Elizabeth Spence
1782      Becomes *White Hart*

---

*Three Legs Of Mann* Wood Street

1820–74      H. Midgley (W. King in Lancaster Inns & Public Houses folder)
[Noted by Richard Bond as closed within his lifetime (1820–91)]

***Three Mariners*** (Beerhouse)                                                 Bridge Lane

This inn, now inextricably confused with the ***Carpenters' Arms***, to which its name has been given, stood in Bridge Lane. It is first mentioned as early as 1722, in John Yeats' will. A sale plan of 1754 is to be found in LCC Deeds, from which its location, sharing a plot with the Old Custom House, is apparent.

| | |
|---|---|
| 1722 | Mentioned in John Yeats' will |
| 1722–1750s | (E. Kennerley; Library MS 8783) |
| 1754 | (Plan in LCC Deeds) |
| 1796 | John Fallows (Library MS 3706) |
| 1820–74 | T. Crossley (W. King in Inns & Public Houses folder) |
| 1864–65 | William Bond (1865 Election Petition) |

[Noted by Richard Bond as closed within his lifetime (1820–91)]

---

***Three Mariners*** (formerly the ***Carpenters' Arms***)                        Bridge Lane

| | |
|---|---|
| 2006 | Mitchell's of Lancaster (Brewers) Ltd. |

Sign of the *Three Mariners*,
Bridge Lane, painted by
Frank Perkins.

---

***Three Pidgeons***                                                                ?

| | |
|---|---|
| 1756 | John Walker (Rental of Fee Farm Rents, Borough Records, Book 'G') |

---

***Three Squirrels*** (see also ***Cock***)                                      North Road

(Predecessor to ***Ship Inn***)
(Cross Fleury, *Time-Honoured Lancaster*, 1891, 454)

## Three Tuns
China Street

This stood in China Lane and has been confused with the *Spink Bull*. (J.R. Spalding, Notes in Library) However, they were clearly separate. It is first recorded in 1772 and last in 1864. It is one of those noted by Richard Bond as closed within his lifetime (1820–91), long before the demolition of much of the old China Lane in the mid-1890s.

| | |
|---|---|
| 1772 | (E. Kennerley; Library MS 8783) |
| 1792 | George Spearman (Stallenge Rolls) |
| 1794 | James Ripley |
| 1818–33 | Richard Thompson |
| 1834 | Robert Stubbs |
| 1837 | To let (*Lancaster Gazette*, 4/11/1837) |
| 1838 | For sale, with Edward Lofthouse tenant |
| 1844 | Edward Barber |
| 1851 | Ann Clark |
| 1856 | John Wilcock |
| 1864–65 | William Lawson (1865 Election petition) |

## Three Tuns
Wood Street

| | |
|---|---|
| 1756–74 | (E. Kennerley; Library MS 8783) |
| 1756 | R. Gibson |
| 1766 | J. Batty |

## Three Tuns
Bridge Lane

| | |
|---|---|
| 1796? | (E. Kennerley; Library MS 8783) |

## Till's Arms (Beerhouse)
Chapel Street

| | |
|---|---|
| 1820–74 | S. Till (W. King in Lancaster Inns & Public Houses folder) |
| 1849–52 | Sarah Till (K. Greenhalgh's notes in Library) |

## Tramway Hotel
127 St Leonardgate

Named after the Lancaster & District Tramway, a horse-drawn system which commenced from Stonewell nearby, this stands on the south side of St Leonardgate. It occupies a much earlier Georgian house. First recorded as an inn in 1895 it was closed and disused by the mid-1980s and has stood derelict since that time. Its etched glass door is in the City Museum. The surviving inn sign shows an electric tramcar, not a horse-drawn one.

| | |
|---|---|
| 1895 | (Election petition) |
| 1896–1901 | R. Veevers |
| 1913 | E. Makinson |
| 1929 | ? |
| 1934 | Anne Makinson |
| 1956–57 | ? |
| 1970 | A. J. Butler |
| 1980s | Closed and disused |

Former *Tramway Hotel*, St Leonardgate.

## Traveller's Rest (Beerhouse)
Penny Street

| | |
|---|---|
| 1865 | Ellershaw (Election Petition) |

## Tubs (see Rose & Crown or Dale's Vaults)
James Street

## Union Flag
Church Street

| | |
|---|---|
| –1779 | (E. Kennerley; Library MS 8783) |
| 1779 | Francis Lonsdall |

## Vanguard
Bridge Lane/St George's Quay

1820–1874  James Townson (W. King in Lancaster Inns & Public Houses folder)
[Noted by Richard Bond as closed within his lifetime (1820–91)]


## Varsity
George Street

Recent
2006  Barracuda Bars Co. Ltd.


## The Vaults (see Cable Street Vaults)
42 Cable Street

1889–90  R. Taylor
1896–1901  J. Allen


## Victoria Hotel
2 West Road

One of the new late-Victorian breed of 'respectable' hotels in the suburbs, this stands in
West Road at the junction with Willow Lane. In 1890 William Mitchell gained its licence by
agreeing to close the *Hole in the Wall* in China Lane, an inn obnoxious to the magistrates and
Corporation.
1890  Built
1896–1913  Isaac R. Jackson
1929  ?
1934  H. Jackson


## Victoria
Penny Street

1820–71  J. Sly (W. King in Inns & Public Houses folder)
1842  J. Sly (to let, *Preston Chronicle*, 27/8/1842)
1844–51  James Wilkinson
–1854  John Waters sen.
1854  John Waters jun.
1864  William Swarbrick
1870  Application for new license (*Lancaster Guardian*, 27/8/1870)
1889–90  W. Bell?
[Noted by Richard Bond as closed within his lifetime (1820–91)]

## Volunteer

This inn stood about halfway along the east side of China Lane. It began in about 1810 and was kept for some thirty-eight years by members of the Boddan family. It later belonged to Yates & Jackson, brewers, who closed it in 1890 in return for a license for the *Park Hotel*.

| | |
|---|---|
| 1810 | (E. Kennerley; Library MS 8783) |
| 1818–34 | Robert Bodden or Boddan |
| 1844 | Ellen Bodden |
| 1851 | Ellen and Jane Boddan |
| –1854 | Ellen Boddan |
| 1854 | James Townson |
| 1855 | Ann Wilkinson |
| 1864–65 | Thomas Procter (1865 Election Petition) |
| 1871–72 | Edward Lievaley |
| 1881 | John Willacy |
| 1886 | John Green |
| 1889–90 | G. Lockhart |

Closed 1890 by Yates & Jackson in return for license for *Park Hotel*
(Gone by 1892 OS)

## Wagon & Horses (Beerhouse)

This was originally a beerhouse. It stands on St George's Quay near the Custom House and consists of the original inn and an adjacent house taken in later, both Georgian. It appears first in 1881, although as is the case with many beerhouses, the origin may be earlier and unrecorded.

| | |
|---|---|
| 1881–96 | Edward G. Maund (1881 census; 1895 Election petition) |
| 1901 | T. Woodhouse |
| 1913 | J. E. Harford |
| 1929 | ? |
| 1934 | J. E. Huck |
| 1933–66 | S. Benson |
| 1966–85? | L. and E. Fisher |
| 1970 | L. Fisher |
| 2006 | Frederick Robinson Ltd. |
| 2008 | Extensively refurbished into garages behind |

*Wagon & Horses*, St George's Quay.

## Walkabout
Dalton Square

Recent
2006        Regent Inns plc

## Warpers' Arms (is this the *Slip Inn?*)
James Street

1820–74     H. Pilkington (W. King in Lancaster Inns & Public Houses folder)
1851–65     Henry Pilkington (1865 Election petition)
[Noted by Richard Bond as closed within his lifetime (1820–91)]

## Waterwitch
Canal Bank opp. Aldcliffe Road

Recent
1980s       Yates Wine Lodge
2002        Westmoreland Brewery
2006        C2 Investment Ltd.
2007        Mitchells

## Wellington (Arms)
8 Common Garden Street

This inn, which stood on the north side of Common Garden Street, at the corner of James Street, first appears in 1816. This is not surprising, given the Duke of Wellington's great victory at Waterloo in the summer of 1815, which made him a national hero. Some tokens bearing the name 'The Iron Duke', a name otherwise unknown in Lancaster, could point to an alternative name for the inn. In 1962 the *Wellington* was demolished as part of the remodelling of the Market and the building of an Arndale Centre.

1816        (E. Kennerley; Library MS 8783)
1816        James Hill
1818–22     John Bowskel or Bouskil
1825–34     Bryan Cornthwaite
1836        For sale, Mrs Cornthwaite tenant (*Lancaster Gazette*, 26/11/1836)
1844        John Wardley
1851–54     Thomas Morland
1854        Mrs Ann Wilkinson
1855        John Wearden
1864–65     John Fisher (1865 Election Petition)
1881        Robert Wolfenden
1886–1901   J. R. Walling
1913        R. Walling
1929        ?
1934        James Hunt
1956–57     ?
1962        Demolished

## Wheatsheaf
James Street

| | |
|---|---|
| 1772 | John Batson (Egerton MS, John Rylands Library) |
| 1778–90 | Robert Gibson, will (LRO, WRW/A 1790) |
| 1794 | Giles Townshend |
| 1818–25 | William Hodgson |

## Wheatsheaf
35 Penny Street

This stood on the east side of Penny Street. It is first listed in 1818. In 1958–59 it was demolished and the site reused.

| | |
|---|---|
| 1818–25 | H. Garnett |
| 1828 | Margaret Garnett |
| 1834–51 | Robert Hinde, will (LRO WRW/A 1854) |
| 1851–56 | Richard Baynes or Baines |
| 1864 | John Morland |
| 1865–72 | James Patterson (1865 Election Petition) |
| 1881–90 | Roger Dugdale |
| 1896–1901 | W. Lancaster |
| 1913 | Elizabeth Beck |
| 1929–34 | W. Cowen |
| 1956–57 | ? |
| 1958–59 | Demolished |

## White Bull
Market Street

| | |
|---|---|
| 1707 | (Kennerley 1982, 6) |
| 1731 | J. Williams (probate: Library MS 2476) |
| 1712–64 | (E. Kennerley; Library MS 8783) |
| 1764– | (Library MSS 2475–84, 2488–2508 inc. lease and release of 1764 (MSS 2477–8)) refer to property 'formerly called Houghton-house, but now known by the name of the White Bull'. Soon after pulled down and converted to houses. |
| 1779 | (J. R. Spalding, Notes in Library) |
| 1879 | Temperance Hotel. (Library MS 2505) |

**White Cross** (later *Farmers' Arms* now *Penny Street Bridge*)          126 Penny Street

The original site of this ancient inn was in Penny Street, next door to the *Corporation Arms* (qv). When the southern approach to the town was altered in 1901 these two inns were demolished and given new sites, the *White Cross* on the west side of King Street, at the corner of Aldcliffe Lane. It was first recorded in 1713. Many of the early references, from 1753–95, are in the Stallenge Rolls, and there is just a possibility that they are referring to an area name rather than the inn specifically. A photograph in the City Museum shows this inn and the *Prince William Henry* in 1865. A sale catalogue for 1899 is in the Library (Library S 1/41). In 1901–2 it was rebuilt on its new site. There is a long overlap in trade directories from 1913 onwards between the names *White Cross* and *Farmers' Arms*. It is possible that the old name stuck long after renaming.

| | |
|---|---|
| 1713 | (Tyldesley Diary) |
| 1713 | (E. Kennerley; Library MS 8783) |
| 1753–55 | John Blacow (Stallenge Rolls) |
| 1776–80 | Richard Farrada (Stallenge Rolls) |
| 1777–78 | George Gill (Stallenge Rolls) |
| 1782–84 | Mrs Dade (Stallenge Rolls) |
| 1785–87 | Richard Dade (Stallenge Rolls) |
| 1785–89 | Richard Ward (Stallenge Rolls) |
| 1788–89 | James Parkinson (Stallenge Rolls) |
| 1792–93 | Thomas Salt (Stallenge Rolls) |
| 1794–95 | Robert Mackay (Stallenge Rolls) |
| 1807 | James Foster (*Lancaster Gazette*, 26/8/1807) |
| 1818–1827 | Thomas Booth, will (LRO WRW/A 1827) |
| 1828 | Ellen Booth |
| 1834 | Edward Kilshaw |
| ? | Billhead for Thexton's (**White Cross & Packet Boat**); (Library Scrapbook 4, pt 1) |
| 1844 | Thomas Thexton |
| 1851 | Henry Row |
| 185? | Joseph Norman |
| –1854 | Jane Norman |
| 1854 | Hezekiah Jemmison or Jamieson |
| 1855–64 | John Hinde |
| c.1865 | photograph in Museum |
| 1871–72 | Mary Hindle |
| 1881 | Robert Wilkinson |
| 1886–96 | John Thompson |
| 1899 | Sale catalogue |
| 1901–2 | Rebuilt on new site |
| 1913 | Margaret Veevers |
| 1929 | ? |
| 1934 | J. E. Raybould |
| 1956–57 | ? |
| 1970 | F. Hanson |

**White Cross**                                                                Quarry Road

Recent
2006         T.J.Tomlinson


**White Hart** (Mistake for the inn in Church Street?)                 Market Street

1752–1808     (E.Kennerley; Library MS 8783)


**White Hart** (see also *Thistle & Crown*)                            58 North Road

This old inn stood on the west side of North Road, at the corner of Church Street. It is first
recorded in 1752. At the rear of the premises, in a yard off Calkeld Lane, was a well which
supplied water used for the inn's brewing. In 1825 the following carriers left from here: John
Sedgwick for Bentham every Tuesday and Friday, Thomas Varey for Burton in Kendal every
Wednesday and Saturday, Anthony Howson for Burton in Lonsdale every Tuesday and
Saturday, and William Goth for Dent every Friday. (Baines' Directory) By 1833 Sedgwick's
route was being operated by Thomas and John Bentham, who also carried goods to Settle and
Leeds. In 1902 the inn was closed and its license transferred to the *Bowerham Hotel*.

1752          Nicholas Atkinson
1772          James Leech (Egerton MS, John Rylands Library)
1779–85       Matthew Geldart (Stallenge Rolls)
1786–87       Mrs Geldart (Stallenge Rolls)

Former *White Hart*, North Road, some time between 1892 and 1901. (Lancaster Library)

| 1794 | William Kews |
|---|---|
| 1802–3 | Benjamin Morris (*Lancaster Gazette*, 18/4/1803) |
| 1803 | for sale |
| 1818–22 | Richard Bullock |
| 1825–28 | Betty Tatham |
| 1834 | John Preston |
| 1838 | John Calvert, sale at inn (*Lancaster Gazette*, 4/8/1838) |
| 1844–49 | Richard Parkinson, will (LRO WRW/A 1848 and 1849) |
| 1851–56 | John Atkinson Bibby |
| 1864 | Richard Richmond |
| 1871–72 | Thomas Smith |
| 1881–86 | Alice Bradley (1881 census) |
| 1889–90 | R.W. Knowles |
| 1892–1901 | W. Richardson |
| 1902 | License transferred to *Bowerham Hotel* |

---

### White Horse (later *Stonewell Tavern*, then *Paddy Mulligan's*, now *Stonewell Tavern* again)      8–12 Church Street

This inn stands on the north side of Lower Church Street, occupying two older buildings, one of which is a rare surviving seventeenth-century building. It began life in about 1806. In 1982 it became the *Stonewell Tavern* and then, in the 1990s, was renamed *Paddy Mulligan's*, as part of the fashion for Irish-themed fun-pubs. Its recent renaming (2005) perhaps signals the end of that particular fashion.

| 1806–23? | (E. Kennerley; Library MS 8783) |
|---|---|
| 1818 | James Tatham |
| 1822 | E. Tatham |
| 1825–34 | Miles Hawthornthwaite |
| 1853 | Mrs Miller |
| 1864 | William Swarbrick |
| 1865 | Jackson (Election Petition) |
| 1866 | John Morland |
| 1871–72 | Matthew Helme |
| 1881–96 | James Helme (1881 census) |
| 1901 | Mrs E. Helme |
| 1913 | W. Elner |
| 1929 | ? |
| 1934 | A.C. Twinn |
| 1956–57 | ? |
| 1982 | Became *Stonewell Tavern* |

*White Horse/Stonewell Tavern*, Church Street.

### White Lion (later *Queen's Hotel*)            3 Penny Street

Situated on the east side of Penny Street, just next door to the *Bear & Staff*, this inn is first mentioned in 1757 when its landlord, Joseph Bainbridge was listed in the Militia Ballot List. Under two landladies, Mary Ellershaw in 1804 and Martha Sowerby in 1822, its contents were itemised by the bailiffs of the Borough Court (Rule Book, 1784–1822, 76 and 168–70). In 1825 the following carriers left from here: Bryan Edmondson and Robert Cornthwaite every Monday, Wednesday and Saturday for Hornby, John Butler and William Pool every Tuesday and Friday as the tides permitted for Ulverston, Thomas Freers every Saturday for Warton, and Thomas Smith and John Dugdale every Saturday for Wray. In 1853 it was rebuilt on the same site and in *c*.1870 its name was changed to *Queen's Hotel*. In 1936–37 this and the *Bear & Staff* were demolished to make way for Woolworths new store.

| | |
|---|---|
| 1757 | Joseph Bainbridge (Militia Ballot List) |
| 1762 | Joseph Bainbridge (E. Kennerley; Library MS 8783) |
| 1775–79 | Richard Allan (Christening of s of Richard Allan, innkeeper, Lancaster PRs 1779) |
| 1782–88 | William Ellershaw (Stallenge Rolls; will in LRO, WRW/A 1788) |
| 1788–92 | Mrs Ellershaw (Stallenge Rolls) |
| 1794 | Stanley Turners |
| to 1803 | Ann Turner |
| 1803–4 | Mary Ellershaw (dr. of above) (*Lancaster Gazette*, 28/5/1803) Bankrupt |
| 1818 | Southern's |
| 1821 | Mrs Martha Sowerby (Library Scrapbook 6, pt 2, 39v) Bankrupt. Inn for sale by auction, *Lancaster Gazette*, 11/5/1822) |
| 1823 | William Powell, will (LRO WRW/A Ad 1824) |
| 1823–37 | Mrs Jane Powell |
| 1844 | Thomas Powell |
| 1851 | John Cawson |
| 1853 | Rebuilt on same site |
| 1853–55 | Isaac Shepherd |
| 1855 | James Hume |
| 1864–65 | Peter Moore (1865 Election Petition) |

(Thereafter see *Queen's*)

---

### White Lion            3 St Leonardgate

Although the building still stands at the north east-end of St Leonardgate it is no longer an inn. For many years it was the tollbar for goods coming into Lancaster from the north east, a function which it shared at other entrance points with the *White Cross* and the *Bridge Inn* (qv). The records often confuse this inn with the *White Lion* in Penny Street (qv). It certainly existed in the late eighteenth century. In 1825 the carrier N. Metcalf left from here every Thursday for Hawes and Richmond. A valuation of 1883 survives in the City Museum. In 1886 the borough tolls were bought out by Lord Ashton, which must have had a dramatic effect upon takings at the inn. In 2002 the *White Lion* was closed and turned into student accommodation.

| | |
|---|---|
| 1762 | Joseph Bainbridge (Hewitson, Memoranda, I, 67) |
| 1772 | John Parkinson (Egerton MS, John Rylands Library) |
| 1794 | John Leice |

Former *White Lion*,
St Leonardgate.

| | |
|---|---|
| 1807 | James Burkit (*Lancaster Gazette*, 26/8/1807) |
| 1818–28 | Richard Leak or Leack |
| 1834 | Thomas Kellet Mashiter |
| 1844–51 | John Green |
| 1856 | William Hill |
| 1864–72 | William Butterworth (1865 Election petition) |
| 1881 | (Census) Dorothy Thomas |
| 1883–85 | Charles Bond |
| 1886 | Tolls bought out by Lord Ashton |
| 1886–96 | Frederick George Nield |
| 1901 | Mrs C. Nield |
| 1901 | (Census) Sarah Ellen Nield |
| 1913 | A. N. Jackson |
| 1929 | ? |
| 1934 | T. Seed |
| 1956–57 | ? |
| 1970 | E. Riley |
| 2002 | Closed and turned into student accommodation |

---

### White Swan (or possibly *Swan With Two Necks*)      St Nicholas Street

| | |
|---|---|
| 1809–10 | (E. Kennerley; Library MS 8783) |
| 1820–74 | No landlord given (W. King in Inns & Public Houses folder) |
| 1804 | Robert Harrison (*Lancaster Gazette*, 23/8/1804) |
| 1850 | R. Harrison (J. R. Spalding, Notes in Library) |
| 1854 | William Dickinson |
| 1857 | Mary Dickinson |

**Wild Boar** (see **Bird in Hand**) Penny Street

1820–74 W. Thompson (source W. King in Lancaster Inns & Public Houses folder)
1859 (*Lancaster Guardian*, 23/7/1859)
[Noted by Richard Bond as closed within his lifetime (1820–91)]

**William IV** Penny Street

[Noted by Richard Bond as closed within his lifetime (1820–91)]

**Yorkshire House** (Beerhouse) 2 Parliament Street

Originally a beerhouse, this stands on the south side of Parliament Street, near the former
Waring & Gillow showrooms and works. It is first recorded in 1853 when its landlord was James
Warbrick. The name may have come from its clientele, as this would be the main road in from
Yorkshire for cattle-drovers and the like.

1853 James Warbrick (*Lancaster Guardian*, 3/9/1853)
–1855 Richard Howson
1855–65 Thomas Jackson (1865 Election Petition)
1871–72 John Lamb
1881–96 John D. Bradley (1881 census; 1895 Election petition)
1901 (Census) Mrs Annie Bradley
1913 W. J. Hall
1929 ?
1934 Agnes Dixon Hall
1956–57 ?
1970 G. F. Beacham
2003 Alison Baxter
2006 Mitchell's of Lancaster (Brewers) Ltd.

*Yorkshire House*, Parliament Street.

# Innkeepers who cannot be assigned to an inn

This list should be read in conjunction with the Gazetteer, which lists all known landlords of known establishments.

| Name | Inn or beerhouse | Place | Source |
|------|------------------|-------|--------|
| Akin, William | I | | Apprentice Rolls 1731 |
| Askew, Edward | B | George Street | Mannex 1851 |
| Askew, George | B | Damside Street | Mannex 1851 |
| Askew, Thomas | I | | LRO WRW/A 1750 |
| Bainbridge, William | I | | LRO WRW/A 1758 |
| Barker, Robert | I | | Apprentice Rolls 1745 |
| Barker, Robert | I | | LRO WRW/A 1776 |
| Beardsworth, Mr | I | | Tyldesley Diary 1713 |
| Bleasdale, Ellen | I | | Rule Book 1736–84, 34, 1765 |
| Bleazard, Marmaduke | B | | LRO WRW/A 1849 |
| Blezard, Elizabeth | B | Penny Street | Mannex 1851 |
| Blezard, Jane | B | Damside Street | Mannex 1851 |
| Bouskill, John | I | | LRO WRW/A 1838 |
| Bradley, R | I | | Rule Book 1784–1822, 47–50, 1801 |
| Brown, John | I | | LRO WRW/A 1782 |
| Bullman, Benjamin | I | | Rule Book 1784–1822, 129, 1816 |
| Butler, William | I | | LRO WRW/A 1801 |
| Campbell, John | B | Cable Street | Mannex 1851 |
| Capstick, John | I | | LRO WRW/A 1801 |
| Cartmel, Thomas | I | | LRO WRW/A 1769 |
| Cawson, Richard | I | Scotforth | LRO WRW/A 1752 |
| Chambers, Thomas | I | | LRO WRW/A 1816 |
| Crook, Thomas | B | King Street | Mannex 1851 |
| Cutler, Ned | I | | Tyldesley Diary 1713 |
| Davis, Thomas | I | | Rule Book 1784–1822, 83, 1805 |
| Dickinson, Joseph | B | St Leonardgate | Mannex 1851 |
| Dickinson, William | B | St Leonardgate | Mannex 1851 |
| Dickson, Thomas | I | | LRO WRW/A 1778 |
| Dixon, Henry | B | St George's Quay | Mannex 1851 |
| Donnoy, Thomas | I | | Apprentice Rolls 1782 |
| Drake, Matthew | I | | Rule Book 1784–1822, 125, 1814 |
| Edmondson, Bryan | B | Wood Street | Mannex 1851 |
| Ellershaw, James | B | Bridge Lane | Mannex 1851 |
| Farra, Will | I | | Tyldesley Diary 1714 |

| Name | Inn or beerhouse | Place | Source |
|---|---|---|---|
| Fell, Margaret | I | | Tyldesley Diary 1714 |
| Hall, William | I | | LRO WRW/A 1749 |
| Hamer, Richard | I | | Rule Book 1784–1822, 118–20, 1813 |
| Harrison, James | B | Penny Street | Mannex 1851 |
| Helme, John | B | Penny Street | Mannex 1851 |
| Herdman, Gawing | I | | LRO WRW/A 1789 |
| Holden, Thomas | B | Skerton | Mannex 1851 |
| Huck, John | I | | Apprentice Rolls 1714 |
| Jackson, Thomas | B | Wood Street | Mannex 1851 |
| Janson, Edward | I | | LRO WRW/A 1780 |
| Kirkham, Arthur | B | St George's Quay | Mannex 1851 |
| Lawson, Richard | I | | LRO WRW/A 1773 |
| Mackarall, George | I | | LRO WRW/A 1778 |
| Mansergh, Will | I | | Tyldesley Diary 1714 |
| Marshall, Thomas | I | | LRO WRW/A 1756 |
| Norman, Joseph | B | King Street | Mannex 1851 |
| Pilling, William | I | | LRO WRW/A 1841 |
| Reynolds, Joseph | I | | Library MS 3783, 1804 |
| Rigby, P | I | | Rule Book 1784–1822, 38, 1797 |
| Riley, James | P | | LRO WRW/A 1840 |
| Smith, Lawrence | I | | Apprentice Rolls 1754 |
| Smith, William | I | | LRO WRW/A 1832 |
| Swann, Lawson | B | Bridge Lane | Mannex 1851 |
| Taylor, James | B | Skerton | Mannex 1851 |
| Thompson, Hannah | B | Church Street | Mannex 1851 |
| Thompson, James | I | | LRO WRW/A 1790 |
| Thompson, Joseph | B | Penny Street | Mannex 1851 |
| Tomlinson, Richard | I | | LRO WRW/A 1783 |
| Wailes, Henry | I | | Tyldesley Diary 1712 |
| Wilson, William | B | St Leonardgate | Mannex 1851 |
| Winder, Thomas | I | | LRO WRW/A 1787 |
| Wood, Edward | B | Skerton | Mannex 1851 |
| Yeats, Samuel | I | | LRO WRW/A 1774 |
| Young, John | I | | LRO WRW/A 1803 |

# *Bibliography*

## *Abbreviations*

CRO     Cumbria Record Office, Barrow-in-Furness
LRO     Lancashire Record Office, Preston
Library    Lancaster Central Library, Local Collection
John Rylands Library John Rylands Library, Manchester

## *Documents*

Census Enumerators' Returns 1841, 1851, 1861, 1871, 1881, 1891 and 1901, in microfilm at Lancaster Library or accessible via AncestryLibrary.com

Hewitson Memoranda, vols 1 and 2. Press cuttings of articles in Lancaster Library

K. R. Greenhalgh's MS notes in Lancaster Library

K. R. Greenhalgh, *Georgian Inns of Lancaster*, 1990. Lancaster Library, PT1576

E. Kennerley, Notes on Corporation, Buildings and Inns. Lancaster Library, MS 8783

W. King, MS List of Lancaster Inns & Public Houses, 1820–74 (City Museum) (This may derive in part from Richard Bond's notes)

Ye Olde Cross Keys, (pamphlet), nd, Lancaster Library PT1046

Lancaster Borough Records; Apprentice Rolls

Lancaster Borough Records; Stallenge Rolls

Lancaster Borough Records; Rule Books 1736–84 and 1784–1823

Lancaster Borough Records; LCC Deeds

J. R. Spalding's MS notes in Library, PT8999

William Stewardson's MS valuation book 1876–77 (City Museum, LM99.1)

At the time of writing (April 2009), much of the manuscript collection held in Lancaster Library is in the process of transfer to the Lancashire Record Office in Preston. Future researchers on this subject are therefore directed to the LRO.

# Books and Journals

E. Baines, *History and Directory of Lancashire*, 1825

M. Blundell, *A Lancashire Squire: The Life of Nicholas Blundell of Crosby 1669–1737*, 2002

R. Bond, 'Memories of seventy years', *Lancaster Philosophical Society Trans.*, 1891

G. Brandwood, A. Davison and M. Slaughter, *Licensed to Sell; the History and Heritage of the Public House*, 2004

P. Clark, *The English Alehouse; a Social History 1200–1830*, 1983

'Cross-Fleury', *Time-Honoured Lancaster*, 1891

G. Fandrey (ed.), *The Craggs of Greenbank*, nd but *c.*1974

E. Garnett, *The Dated Buildings of South Lonsdale*, CNWRS, 1994

J. Gillow and A. Hewitson (eds), *The Tyldesley Diary: Personal Records of Thomas Tyldesley during the years 1712–13–14*, 1873

J. S. Hayes and A. J. Noble (eds), *The 1757 Militia Ballot List for South Lonsdale, (Lancashire)*, Lancaster City Museums, 1997

A. Hillman (transc.), *The Rake's Diary; Journal of George Hilton*, 1994

E. Kennerley, 'Old Inns and Public Houses in Lancaster', *Lonsdale Historical Society Trans.*, 1982, 5–10

E. Kennerley, 'The social importance of the inns and alehouses of Lancaster in the eighteenth and nineteenth centuries', *CNWRS Regional Bulletin*, 3, 1989

E. Kennerley, 'Lancaster Inns and Alehouses 1600–1730', *Lancashire Local Historian*, 5, 1990, 40–51

*Lancaster Election Commission 1866, Report of Proceedings from September 27 to October 28 1866* (reprinted from *Lancaster Guardian*)

*Lancaster Borough Election: Minutes of Evidence taken before the Select Committee on the Lancaster Borough Election Petition*, 1866

*Lancaster Election Petition against the return of Col. Foster MP*, 1896

J. Larwood & J C Hotten, *English Inn Signs*, 1951

*Leaves from Local History* (Extracts from *Lancaster Gazette*, 1801-50), 1865

*Universal British Directory*, 1794

A. White (ed.), *A History of Lancaster*, 2001

A. White, *Lancaster: A History*, 2003

A. White, *Life in Georgian Lancaster*, 2004

Some of the Rule Books, the Stallenge Rolls and other Borough Records are currently available on CD from the City Museum

# The Sun Hotel & Bar

## *One of Lancaster's most historic inns*

Established 1684

❝ The Sun Hotel & Bar is recognised as one of the
finest bars in the United Kingdom, achieving nine
national and local awards since opening in 2003.
Our sixteen ensuite rooms are in keeping with
our hotel's national reputation and offer luxury
accomodation in the heart of Lancaster city centre ❞

63-65 Church Street, Lancaster LA1 1ET

info@thesunhotelandbar.co.uk   01524 66006   www.thesunhotelandbar.co.uk

A modern twist on a traditional coaching inn and the perfect venue
for the launch of *Lancaster's Historic Inns*